HAPPINESS RESCUE

How to be Happy, Find your Passion,
and Live Life to the Fullest

AMANDA MAY STARK

Copyright © 2018 Amanda May Stark. All rights reserved.

No part of this book may be reproduced by any mechanical, photographic, or electronic process, or in the form of a phonographic recording; nor may it be stored in a retrieval system, transmitted, or otherwise be copied for public or private use, other than for "fair use" as brief quotations embodied in articles and reviews, without prior written permission of the publisher or author.

This book is for educational and informational purposes only. The author does not dispense medical advice or prescribe the use of any technique as a form of treatment for physical or mental problems without the advice of a physician or mental health professional, either directly or indirectly. The intent of the author is only to offer information of a general nature to help you in your quest for emotional and spiritual well-being.

Because of the dynamic nature of the Internet, web addresses or links contained in this book may have changed since publication and may no longer be valid. The views expressed in this work are solely those of the author and do not necessarily reflect the view of the publisher, and the publisher hereby disclaims any responsibility for them.

Cover design: Kelsey Souchereau
Editor: Kate Allyson
Formatter: Leila Summers

First Edition 2018

ISBN: 978-1-9995213-0-1

Published by Amanda May Stark, Stark Marketing Services Ltd.

TABLE OF CONTENTS

INTRODUCTION 1

CHAPTER ONE 7
Happiness Starts with a Smile

CHAPTER TWO 12
Let Go of The Past

CHAPTER THREE 18
Ditch the Drama

CHAPTER FOUR 23
Blaming & Complaining

CHAPTER FIVE 28
Life's Expectations

CHAPTER SIX 33
Colour Outside the Lines

CHAPTER SEVEN 40
Step Outside Your Comfort Zone

CHAPTER EIGHT 46
Get Out of Your Rut

CHAPTER NINE 52
Confront the Escape Artist

CHAPTER TEN 58
Just Quit Procrastinating

CHAPTER ELEVEN 62
A Self-Empowered Mindset

CHAPTER TWELVE 69
Wiping Out Limiting Beliefs

CHAPTER THIRTEEN 75
The Comparison Trap

CHAPTER FOURTEEN 82
Set Your Goal and Establish Rituals

CHAPTER FIFTEEN 90
Think Small to Achieve Big

CHAPTER SIXTEEN 97
To Do Lists Fail, Success Lists Soar

CHAPTER SEVENTEEN 104
Love Yourself Mindfully

CHAPTER EIGHTEEN 112
Make It Happen with Visualization

CHAPTER NINETEEN 120
Your Lifestyle Shift

CHAPTER TWENTY 128
Finding Gratitude

CHAPTER TWENTY-ONE 136
Learn to Laugh Again
CHAPTER TWENTY-TWO 142
Drop the Crutch
CHAPTER TWENTY-THREE 149
Rediscover Your Passion
CHAPTER TWENTY-FOUR 154
Branching Out
CHAPTER TWENTY-FIVE 161
Let Your Inner Child Out to Play
AFTERWORD 165
CONTINUE YOUR HAPPINESS RESCUE WITH ME! 168
REDISCOVER YOUR PASSION WORKSHEET 173
ACKNOWLEDGEMENTS 178
ABOUT THE AUTHOR 181

This book is dedicated to those who have spent their life going through the motions: those looking after everyone else around them, and who long for something more. Life has its ups and downs and how we handle them can either define or destroy us.

Happiness Rescue is your go-to resource to reflect, recreate, and rise above whatever challenge(s) you are facing. I am proud to be a survivor. A survivor of defeat, bullying, self-sabotage, and neglect. I now live my life with true conviction, honesty, peace, and joy.

I dedicate this book to all the survivors who will follow me. To face your fears, overcome your insecurities, and to decide to make your passion, purpose and happiness a priority in your life.

Amanda ox

INTRODUCTION

"It is during our darkest moments that we must focus to see the light."
~ Buddha ~

I had no idea that today would be the day that everything changed. I couldn't believe it. What should have been a very exciting time in my life was turning out to be one of the most challenging experiences I have ever had.

The day before, my online business-coaching contract suddenly crashed and there was no way to recover any money, commissions, or clients from the business. My husband and I had invested a lot of time and money into the company. I was doing incredible things with my wonderful clients and now it was all stripped away, just like that! That same night I had gone to my future daughter-in-law's bachelorette party for a paint night and dinner, which I was not in the mood for. All I wanted was to curl up and cry. I drowned my pain in margaritas and painted a very miserable painting, the opposite of the beautiful sunset everyone else was painting. Inside, I felt like I wanted to die.

I woke up the next day feeling empty and slightly hungover. Today was supposed to be another incredible monumental day. Instead it turned into my lowest point where I hit rock bottom. It was my son's bachelor party celebration where most of the men I love, including my husband and 2 sons, were all headed out of town to play paintball and go "clubbing" at a popular dance bar for an overnight adventure.

When my husband left the house at 11:30 a.m., I was still in bed. He kissed me good-bye and I was alone. For the whole day I was immobilized, stuck in bed, in the dark, contemplating the value of my life. I was numb and entirely alone, except for my dogs. I felt sad, lonely, abandoned, useless, disposable and unlovable. I lay there all day until my dogs wouldn't stop staring at me. Regardless of how I felt, they wanted their walk.

Even though I felt horrible, I still felt bad about not walking my dogs. So, I dragged my butt out of bed, got dressed, put my shoes on, got the leash and harnesses ready, and out we went. It was lovely outside, but even my dogs couldn't switch my mood. I only made it down the end of the block, where I sat down on a park bench. For a while I just sat there. Nothing was working. I felt like I could just disappear and no one would notice that I was gone. We walked back to the house. My only motivation was a nail appointment. I didn't want to disappoint my manicurist, but I really didn't feel like going.

After my nail appointment, I went back to bed with my dogs. I didn't even care enough to eat dinner. For the first time in my life, I had thoughts that the world would be better off without me, and I was worthless and a failure. With everything I had been through, I felt like I was about to explode! With all of my problems, my insecurities, my failures, and my faults, who would really want to be around me?

My husband got back around noon the next day. I was still in bed when he got home. When I saw him, I just cried. I had survived that night, thanks to my dogs and my nail appointment, but I knew that never in my life had I felt so weak, miserable, and sad.

What ultimately saved me was the fact that I couldn't hurt those around me. My husband, my sons, my parents, and my friends would be devastated. I would rather suffer for the rest of my life than make them suffer for the rest of theirs. That day, I opened up to my husband. The day after, I booked a doctor's appointment. It was time I took ownership of my life, if I was going to have a life.

My doctor's appointment was 2 weeks later. I was anxious about it, but also looking forward to it. I opened up and shared anything I could think of. I shared everything about my life, including my behaviour, my diet, my alcohol consumption, my business, and my worst day. After a lengthy discussion and some tests, the doctor told me what I had already suspected for years; that I had depression. She prescribed an antidepressant medication and said, "I want you to understand you have not started feeling like this overnight, and so you won't be feeling super duper overnight either. This will take time and I am here with you the entire way, but we are looking at a minimum of 6 months pending your progress."

Driving home, my mind was clouded with negative thoughts. I was so embarrassed, afraid to be labeled as "depressed" for the rest of my life. What would my family think? With all these thoughts, it was no wonder I was depressed.

About a month later, my son and his fiancé got married. I was really nervous about the wedding, as any mother of the groom would be. After a month of being on the antidepressants, I had stabilized. I had seen a counsellor a few times and I had a more positive mindset. I was meditating daily and being kind and patient with myself. I had adjusted my life to reduce stress, and I was in a much better place where I could enjoy this special occasion.

As it turned out it poured rain for the entire rehearsal and morning of the wedding. We hoped that the ceremony would be moved inside, but my son and his soon-to-be-wife were adamant about having their wedding outdoors. The rest of us thought they were crazy.

As my son's dad and I walked him to the bridge where he would marry his high-school sweetheart, the clouds opened. The sun appeared and shone down for the first time in days. We were all in awe of how beautiful their ceremony was. It was truly magical.

In that moment, I was awakened and discovered my purpose. The universe was giving me a sign to be happy, and to breathe. I decided to re-start my business and direct all of my energies into understanding and promoting happiness. That moment inspired this book. In my darkest moments, I had never imagined I could write a book that would help people. But I found my path and created *Happiness Rescue*.

My goal is to use my experience as a tool to mentor others on how to avoid the hopeless thoughts, negative emotions, and the spiral effects of being stuck, having low confidence, or feeling sadness and depression. I will show you how to re-focus your energies, build your self-confidence, eliminate your limiting beliefs, reduce your bad choices and habits, and reward yourself for small and large accomplishments! Create your own Happiness Rescue and save yourself from even one more day of pain and misery.

So, if you are feeling stuck, lacking passion and purpose, fear failure, or feel sad, then this book will take you back to your happy place. I am not a doctor and I will not be providing you with any medical advice. What I will do is throw a life raft to you, so you can take positive action, and live your life to the fullest!

Throughout this book I have added extra value with free downloadable gifts, products, and links. Look for the Happiness Rescue lifesaver shown here.

Keep reading; take action day-by-day and step-by-step to uncover your purpose and your passion. This book is exactly what you need to unlock the happiness you truly deserve!

The techniques in this book are designed to help you live your best life. However, if you are feeling suicidal, having thoughts that life is not worth living, or thinking that the world would be better off without you, you need professional help. In this case, please contact your doctor or your local emergency services immediately.

Enjoy Happiness Rescue,

Amanda ox

CHAPTER ONE

HAPPINESS STARTS WITH A SMILE

"You're going to realize it one day — that happiness was never about your job, or your degree, or being in a relationship. Happiness was never about following in the footsteps of all of those who came before you, it was never about being like the others. One day, you're going to see it — that happiness was always about the discovery, the hope, the listening to your heart and following it wherever it chose to go. Happiness was always about being kinder to yourself, it was always about embracing the person you were becoming. One day, you will understand. That happiness was always about learning how to live with yourself, that happiness was never in the hands of other people. It was always about you. It was always about you."
~ Bianca Sparacino ~

What does it mean to be happy? For me, happiness starts with a SMILE, which stands for being:

S = Successful
M = Mindful
I = Inspired
L = Loved
E = Empowered

Happiness is an emotion or feeling that we all crave. We all want to be happy and we are all searching for happiness. Yet, no one else can give you happiness. I cannot create happiness for you, but I can show you a path that will lead to a happier life. You can be happy, no matter what your personal situation is, if you decide that happiness is what you want. We all have our own biases and our own opinions on what happiness is. The definition of happiness varies from one person to another. No one else can tell you what happiness means to you.

There are many layers, which can either block or blossom our life happiness. Consider it like an onion working from outside distractions and influences through to the very core, which is our inner happiness. Each of us has our own desires and our own ideas of what it means to be truly happy — yet we all desire happiness in one form or another.

If we all desire happiness, why isn't it easy to find? The truth is that there are many obstacles on our path to happiness, which can include:

- Our past
- Our brain's programming
- Our own and other's negative thoughts and actions
- Our own insecurities
- Patterns of reluctances
- Self-defeating tendencies
- Lack of focus
- Getting in our own way

When you can remove these obstacles, you will find your way to finally loving yourself, which is the key to inner happiness. When we are in a state of happiness, everything changes around us. Our relationships, career, interactions, and our ability to create abundance in our lives all improve when we are happy.

In North America and in most first world countries, the term "happiness" is typically used to describe hedonistic pleasures. "Happiness" comes from outside experiences and is only short-term. For example:

1. You receive a raise at work
2. You win $25,000 in the lottery
3. You eat a bag of your favourite candy

These examples are positive life events and you do deserve to be and feel happy. The problem is in 6 months time you will feel the same as you do today. Your overall level of happiness has not changed just because of one good external event.

The lasting form of happiness is what we ultimately strive for and that is the focus of this book. For a true Happiness

Rescue, you need to uncover your roadblocks to happiness so that you can experience inner peace, joy, and fulfillment.

Short-term happiness is largely defined as increased pleasure and decreased pain. It revolves around a person's current feelings and emotional state. It can include positive emotions such as pleasure, joy, curiosity, pride, awe, and excitement or negative emotions like anger, shame, guilt, stress, or sadness.

Lasting happiness revolves around a person's satisfaction with their life. It is more reflective of their life experiences and doesn't change when their emotions do. Having a purpose in life, finding meaning, and growing as a person are all a part of lasting happiness.

The difference between short-term and long-term happiness is that one is concerned with transient feelings or emotions; while the other reflects how a person sees their life. Short-term happiness is influenced by moods or daily experiences. Long-term happiness persists despite negative events or emotions.

In Happiness Rescue, I am going to focus on the actions and thoughts that bring long-term happiness. My definition of happiness is not going to be the same as yours, but the techniques I used can help you too. Throughout this book, I will help you discover and define your own version of happiness.

The other key to long-term happiness is understanding that no one else can find it for you. You can be in a wonderful relationship with your partner and you might be very happy in your relationship, but that does not make you a happy person. I love my husband very much and we have a strong love for each other. But if he is not happy, I can't wave a magic wand and help him. He must do the work to find his own happiness and to determine what that is for him.

Remember, happiness starts with a smile:

S = Successful
M = Mindful
I = Inspired
L = Loved
E = Empowered

CHAPTER TWO

LET GO OF THE PAST

"Holding on is believing that there's a past; letting go is knowing that there's a future."
~ Daphne Rose Kingma ~

"Letting go of your painful past is how you open yourself to a wonderful future."
~ Bryant McGill ~

We cannot move forward in our lives if we are holding on to the past. Holding on to what is comfortable, including painful past experiences is human nature. Think about a painful memory — one that you have relived over and over. How do you feel? You probably feel the pain, but you also feel the comfort of familiarity. You *know* this pain, you are comfortable with it, and it's easier to deal with than the unknown pain that might come from a situation that you are experiencing now.

In the early years of my life, I had so much transition. For the first fifteen years, we moved every 2 years due to my father's job. Then for the next fifteen I moved nationally and internationally because of my sport and career. As a result, it was difficult to establish any kind of roots or hang onto any permanent relationships in my life. Moving all the time has had a huge impact not only on my relationships, but also on my self-esteem. I couldn't ever trust anyone explicitly. I was so insecure and therefore I did everything I could to get attention, positive or negative.

We do not want to look back and regret anything we have done, but sometimes what we did do can directly impact how we move forward and how we feel about ourselves. Back then; I was like a toddler who is in her high-chair and being ignored. What does the toddler do? She drops a toy, spoon, Sippy-cup or bangs things making loud noises. She wants attention and doesn't care how she gets it.

At first, I used my sport to get attention. I practiced and received lots of attention when I was doing well. But when it wasn't going so well, that attention went away, and I couldn't handle it. I rebelled: I sought out bad relationships, drank too much alcohol, tried drugs, and did whatever I could to get that attention. I took these behaviours with me when I left home and became an adult. Instead of digging deep when a relationship got difficult, I would rebel to get unnecessary attention, pushing away those who were closest to me.

After retiring from my sport, I was a mother of 2 beautiful young boys and unfortunately, I was going through a divorce. I had to put my "big-girl" pants on and grow up — little humans were depending on me! I changed my attention-seeking behaviour so I could be a positive role model for my boys.

When life closes one door, another one opens, so I went to university and began to build a life for myself. Most recently, my business crashed overnight. I felt depressed for a while, but I realized I had 2 choices: I could go straight back into the past and repeat my attention-seeking behaviour, or I could open my eyes and look at this experience as a thing of the past and move forward.

Holding on to the pain of the past is only hurting you. Maybe you had an opinion that was very valuable to you in the past — holding on to that is okay as long as it's still serving you and is not hurtful or condescending. But sometimes, to move forward, you have to decide that you would rather be happy than be right. Many years ago, my best friend and I had a huge disagreement about some of my past behaviours. She did not approve of my actions and for ten years we did not talk. A couple of years ago, she reached out to me and after an incredible conversation, we decided to let the past be the past. We have since healed our relationship, become more honest with each other and I am so happy she is back in my life!

One day, a professor of psychology began his lecture by grabbing a glass of water. The students waited for the classic question: Is the glass half empty, or half full? But the professor surprised them. He asked, "How heavy is this glass of water?" "6 ounces," called out one student. "Ten ounces," said another. The professor shook his head, then explained:

"The actual weight doesn't matter. What really matters is how long I've been holding it. If I hold it for just a minute, it feels very light. If I hold it for an hour, I'll have an ache in my arm. If I hold it for a whole day, my arm will feel numb and paralyzed. Any longer than that and I will be very tempted to give up and drop it. In each case, the weight of the glass doesn't change, but the longer I hold it, the heavier it becomes.

The stresses and worries in life are like this glass of water. Carry them for only a short while and they're manageable. Worry about them a bit longer and they begin to hurt. And if we think about them all day long, or longer, we can begin to feel paralyzed and hopeless – incapable of concentrating or focusing on anything else.

It's important to remember to let go of your stress whenever possible. As early in the evening as you can, put all your burdens down. Don't carry them through the evening and into the night. This can certainly be easier said than done in some cases, but in many cases it's actually quite easy if we're mindful about it."

The next time you are feeling the weight of the world on your shoulders, remember to put down the glass — don't carry it around like a burden or responsibility.

Here are 3 ways you can let go of the past and move forward:

1. <u>Stop Blaming Yourself</u>
    We all know how to play the blame game! You can dwell on something for days, weeks, months, or even years, doing nothing but blaming yourself. We seem to put a heavy burden on ourselves and fester over what we did, what we could have done better and what we could have changed. But the truth is that this blame is holding you back. Whether you're blaming yourself for a bad grade, a breakup, or for how lost and sad you feel, blaming doesn't help. Instead, focus on learning from this event and think about the future. What will you do next time you're in a similar situation? Letting go of the blame will settle your mind into happy thoughts that bring you peace and joy.

2. <u>Say "Yes" to What Is and Own It</u>
    "Whatever the present moment contains, accept it as if you had chosen it. Always work with it, not against it," Eckhart Tolle says. If you are working against the present moment, you will be unable to move forward. Instead, accept what is, and own it — but don't blame yourself! If someone has hurt you in the past, you can decide whether you want to forgive them or not. But if you choose not to forgive them, accept that as your choice. (See more about forgiveness below.) To begin your Happiness Rescue you must own your story.

3. Forgiveness
There is beauty in every day. But many people are blind to this beauty because of resentment, bitterness, and pent-up anger. When we harbour bad feelings, emotions and grudges for too long, we cannot even *begin* to feel happy. When you feel negative emotions of hatred, anger, avoidance or animosity, recognize them and deal with them immediately. Do not let them fester. We cannot avoid the past, but we no longer need to react to it. Also, forgiveness is not for the person who you are forgiving: it is for yourself. When you forgive, you let go of the anger and hurt that's preventing you from moving forward.

CHAPTER THREE

DITCH THE DRAMA

"A life filled with silly social drama and gossip indicates that a person is disconnected from purpose and lacking meaningful goals. People on a path of purpose don't have time for drama."
~ Brendon Burchard ~

"When you are not honouring the present moment by allowing it to be, you are creating drama."
~ Eckhart Tolle ~

We all have people in our lives that we are excited to be around. People who we have a lot in common with and can easily talk to. When we spend time with these people, we feel energized. On the contrary, there are also people who are the opposite: people who you might have very little in common with or who complain a lot. These people suck the life out of us, causing us to feel drained and exhausted.

We become what we surround ourselves with. If you surround yourself with negative people, you yourself will become a more negative person. The good news is that if you surround yourself with positive, uplifting people, you will also become a positive person who others will want to be around.

People who are continually pessimistic and always looking at the dark side are addicted to drama and it almost gives them a false sense of validity and power. They feel temporarily important and accepted by their peers, society, their community, family or even themselves. On the other hand, people who are optimistic don't need drama to feel confident. They know their worth and don't need to seek acceptance in negative ways.

Drama is a behaviour, which engages people in negative conversations about others, when they have nothing else to contribute. These people struggle to live in the moment and feel the need to complain. They are usually emotionally charged from unresolved personal wounds from the past, which are taken out on others.

Engaging in drama is habit-forming and can be an accessible form of attention getting for the inner toddler. To fit in and feel happy, you must release the need for drama. Drama loves drama and the more you contribute to it, it will only fester and it adds fuel to the fire. With the practice of mindfulness, it is possible to not respond to drama. Mindfulness helps to neutralize drama and the fire fizzles instead of festers.

When I was working in my corporate position, I had the privilege and also challenge of managing a team of 6. I enjoyed the dynamics of the team; however, they were all very good friends before I became their manager. As the manager, I made some budgeting and policy changes to enhance productivity. Unfortunately, this led to laying off staff that could not work the hours of operation required. As the staff were used to working the same hours for years before my appointment, they were very reluctant to change. As a result, our working environment became toxic very quickly. This included: staff talking behind my back and whispering to loyal customers. I felt very hurt and double guessed myself.

I knew I needed to step back from the situation and be their manager, not their friend. To save the business, tough decisions were needed, and I knew what I was doing was right. I was becoming emotionally charged because of my own insecurities and self-doubt as a new manager.

I could not solve their personal pains and feelings by bringing my own emotions into the situation. What I needed to do was practice mindfulness and step into a space of neutrality. A space where my feelings or drama had no impact or electrical charge within the situation.

Since this experience, I have become more successful practicing mindfulness, realizing if I do not respond to drama then the drama ends. Drama loves more drama, pain loves more pain, and negativity loves more negativity.

There are signs you may be addicted to drama. For instance, you frequently find yourself involved in other people's arguments that have literally nothing to do with you. You may also enjoy gossiping about people and situations that you're not involved in. You're constantly complaining about all the drama in your life, because you feel you have nothing else to talk about. And, you talk about the past a lot, without seeing the excitement and opportunities of the now or your future.

How is it possible to not respond to drama? The first step is to recognize drama when it is in front of you. It is also critical to recognize if you are bringing the drama.

Here are 3 practices to implement to resist responding to drama:

1. <u>Observe your body sensations, thoughts, and emotions</u>
   If you notice your heart rate increasing or your face flushing, let that be your cue to physically step away from the situation. Be present with your sensations and use your breath and mindfulness skills to bring you to a state of physical and emotional homeostasis where your muscles are relaxed, and your breath is slow and even. Once the body, thoughts, and emotions are back to neutral, reapproach the situation from a less reactive place.

2. Create some sense of space
   Often when you experience drama it feels like you are being suffocated or being compressed. You may notice yourself holding your breath as lots of people talk at once. Allow yourself space in these situations by focusing internally, taking deep breaths or gazing downward. With each breath you will notice your body starting to relax and so will your desire to feel the tension of the drama unfolding.

3. Become mindful and accept the discomfort
   The most powerful thing you can do to remove drama from your life is to not contribute to it. You do this by not responding, which takes practice. Not responding to it means silence. It means not asking questions that take you deeper into the situation. It means not agreeing or disagreeing, either with words or body language. What you practice will strengthen and get easier with time.

The need for drama comes from jealousy, low-self esteem, thinking you are not good enough, and fear of failing. By not lending energy to something you do not want, you immediately create a closer connection to what you do want. If you want to ditch the drama in your life, drop the drama at the door. If you want more happiness and joy, choose to feel happy and joyful.

CHAPTER FOUR

BLAMING & COMPLAINING

"People won't have time for you if you are always angry or complaining."
~ Stephen Hawking ~

"Be grateful for what you have and stop complaining — it bores everybody else, does you no good, and doesn't solve any problems."
~ Zig Ziglar ~

What do I mean by "blaming and complaining?" Blaming is the act of finding fault with everything around you, without taking any responsibility for your own situation. For example, when my first marriage ended, I could have blamed my husband, and said that we got divorced because of his depression and self-destructive behaviours. But the truth is that I was also responsible: I acted out for attention in unhealthy ways. Instead of focusing on our marriage, I rebelled and engaged in my own self-sabotaging behaviours. I was associating myself with toxic people, obsessively training, staying out late, and doing anything I could to avoid what we were going through as a couple. Blaming others prevents us from seeing our faults and moving forward.

Complaining is expressing unhappiness with a situation, like the person who grumbles every single time it rains. All complaining does is bring up negative energy, without doing anything to solve the situation. This happened to me even when I played squash. When I complained about my opponent when they were late to a match, all it did was make me frustrated and distracted me from playing my own game.

To avoid getting stuck in a negative spiral, it is important to know the source of our pessimism and unhappiness. Blaming and complaining are 2 main sources of our negative habits. Our attraction to these 2 negative sidekicks is unhealthy and detrimental to us as individuals and as a society. Although blaming and complaining may seem like separate actions, in practice they are hard to separate. For instance, it is difficult to complain without an underlying feeling of blame. When you are unhappy or dissatisfied with someone or something, your feelings of negativity lead you to complaining.

Drama cannot exist without blaming and complaining. When we complain about something we push the issue away from ourselves, and put it on someone or something else instead. When we are constantly blaming and complaining, we are being negative, jealous, and envious. We make excuses for the results or lack of results we are getting in our lives. Like drama, blaming and complaining are addictive and once we start unconsciously blaming and complaining, it is very difficult to progress towards any of our goals or to be truly happy in our lives.

When we are blaming and complaining, we are taken over by a victim consciousness. We become the victim of circumstances. In this kind of consciousness, we feel helpless and powerless. We are taken over by our wounded persona and we cannot see things clearly. We believe that the world owes us something, or that our lives would be better if only the situation was different. Furthermore, in this position, nothing ever changes in our lives until we start to take responsibility for what is happening. Negativity attracts negativity. Our happiness transformation is to see what we are doing and own it.

So, how can we stop these negative habits? The first step toward dealing with blaming and complaining is to become aware that we are doing it and realize that it is sabotaging our lives and those we love around us.

In past years, I have gone through many life adversities including a layoff from a corporate management job, major surgery, losing my business, family confrontations, and physical and mental health challenges. Instead of looking inward for solutions to these problems, I just made excuses for everything.

When I got laid off, I went through months of blaming the economy, the recession, other staff, and even myself. I complained about how it could have been avoided, and that I wasn't given the promotion that I had earlier been promised. All these excuses were just allowing me to wallow in misery and negativity, instead of doing what I needed to do — move on!

As I got older, I began experiencing arthritis and joint problems: bone on bone in my knees, hip surgery, and chronic back and neck issues. I have always loved being active and playing competitively, but at this point I was reserved to more gentle exercises with less impact. To me, that meant no more competitive sport. I could still go to the gym, but that seemed so boring. So, instead of taking care of myself, I blamed my genetics, my weight, my doctor, and the pain I was in. All I did was blame and complain instead of taking action.

As I have grown through this process, I have finally discovered how to be happy and stop blaming and complaining. All the bitching would not help my joints, nor would it help me get my job back. Eventually, you just have to lift your chin up and realize that the only way to move forward and to be happy is to decide to stop blaming and complaining!

If you get stuck, here are 7 ways to stop blaming and complaining so you can move forward towards your Happiness Rescue:

1. Release the pain of the past (see Chapter 2).
2. Take responsibility for your life and circumstances.

3. Remember you always have a choice: you can turn things around any time you want.

4. Change your vocabulary: instead of "should" say "choose to," instead of saying "I hope" say "I will," and instead of saying "I'll try" say "I'll do."

5. Learn to say "no."

6. Change your focus from the negative to the positive.

7. Start by taking small steps outside of your comfort zone.

CHAPTER FIVE

LIFE'S EXPECTATIONS

"Remember that sometimes not getting what you want is a wonderful stroke of luck."
~ Dalai Lama ~

"People look to time in expectation that it will eventually make them happy, but you cannot find true happiness by looking toward the future."
~ Eckhart Tolle ~

Expectations create our ultimate life experience. Our expectations can also determine our feelings of disappointment or happiness. They are a list of things we build up in our mind that tell us how things should be. They pull us out of the moment and hold us in an infinite loop of endless possibilities. They are a belief about what might happen in the future, like what our weekend is going to be like. If our weekend does not live up to our expectations, we are disappointed and if it does then we feel happy.

We all have expectations when we go into an event, meet someone new or have an experience. Some people have naturally high expectations and others have low expectations, but ultimately our expectations, whether high or low, can actually block us from happiness.

Imagine a pendulum, which swings from one side to the other. Our daily emotions, moods, interactions and outcomes are like this pendulum. For example, you plan a vacation when you have not had one for a very long time. You plan to stay at a 5-star resort, imagine jumping in the waves, and see yourself sunbathing on the beach. But when you arrive at your destination the hotel is not up to your standards and the weather is rainy the entire time with an incoming hurricane. Your vacation is ruined, you don't get to do the things you were anticipating, and you come home, feeling like you need a vacation from your vacation!

The next vacation you go on, you decide you are just going to approach this one with very low expectations. You take the "I don't really care" attitude and expect the worst. As a result, you make no plans, are in a terrible mood the entire time waiting for bad things to happen, and can't see the positive in anything. Once again, your vacation is ruined.

As an elite athlete I was a perfectionist and had very high expectations of myself. I trained for hours everyday on the court, track, and with my personal trainer. In addition, I mentally prepared with visualization, affirmations, and rituals. For over 15 years, this was all I did, full-time. I was incredibly passionate, dedicated and committed to succeeding. While I had expectations of all my performances, they needed to be realistic. Had I set my expectations too high, I would have become so frustrated and disappointed when I lost, and I doubt my career would have lasted as long as it did. Had I set my expectations too low, I wouldn't have pushed myself, and I wouldn't have trained my hardest or done my best. Once again, my career would not have lasted very long.

What's the solution? If having high expectations ruins the experience when it doesn't live up to them, and having low expectations just makes you miserable the entire time, how can you possibly get through life? My suggestion is to let go of all your expectations. It is okay to still make plans, but understand these plans may change. Maybe you will pleasantly be surprised and feel joy and happiness by letting go. To live a happy, joyful and peaceful life we must let go of our expectations and get real with ourselves. Just allow your life to happen instead of having a preconceived notion of the outcome of a certain situation.

Using visualization and meditation works incredibly well when consciously aware of lowering your expectations. You can also repeat to yourself the mantra I use when I am letting go of control, which is: *breathe, exhale, and happiness will prevail.*

Another way for you to live with realistic expectations is to turn all your shoulds into musts. As soon as you can do this, you stop living your life for others and begin to live your life for yourself. This is incredibly rewarding because you determine your musts and you have more influence and control of them. When we choose should we are choosing it for something or someone else. Our musts are what we believe and what we do when we are alone as our most authentic self. For example, instead of walking my dog because I should, I now say that I must walk my dog for not only her happiness, but for mine as well.

Shoulds create expectations, which unconsciously can creep into our day-to-day lives and affect our overall happiness. Being true to ourselves and focusing on our musts lower our expectations of others and those we have on ourselves. To have no expectations is improbable, but to have realistic expectations, and be able to let go of them when necessary, is where happiness prevails.

Here are 3 ways to set reasonable expectations:

1. Examine closely the expectations you have of yourself
   Trying to get everything done perfectly, all at once will not only prevent you from taking action, but will often leave you feeling depressed and disappointed in your abilities, which can only breed negative self-talk. Instead of berating yourself because you "should" be debt free or you "should" have lost 10 pounds, make a conscious choice to re-evaluate your goal. Unrealistic expectations only prevent you from dealing with the situation and keep you feeling stuck and powerless.

2. Reconsider your expectations of others
   Do you have a mental list of all the things your partner, friends, or co-workers should be doing to make you

happy? If you do, it is time to reconsider the list and begin to focus less on what they are not doing and more on what you can do.

3. Release your expectations of events
Like setting expectations for yourself and others, when you put all of your hopes and dreams into the outcome of a specific event, you are setting yourself up for disappointment. Try to enter events without the cause or outcome you hope to produce.

When you ditch the drama and set realistic expectations for yourself, those people around you, and your life situations, you'll avoid a lot of bumps and bruises that come from disappointment. As you create your Happiness Rescue, you begin to clearly see your habit patterns, thought patterns, and actions that are leading you towards or away from happiness. You'll discover why you are who you are, where you want to be and how you can begin to take proactive steps to feeling inner peace, love and happiness in your life.

CHAPTER SIX

COLOUR OUTSIDE THE LINES

*"You have to colour outside the lines
once in a while if you want to make
your life a masterpiece."*
~ Albert Einstein ~

When my sons were only 4 and 6, I went through a divorce from their father while still playing and coaching squash professionally. The challenge with being an athlete and sport-specific coach was I typically worked when other people did not work. On evenings and weekends, I would be working, teaching lessons and clinics, or traveling to tournaments and events. Even though their dad had an active role in their lives, I felt that working when my young children were home from school was not an ideal life. So, I took the big plunge, enrolled into university and began my bachelor's degree.

As I was a mature student and had been out of school for so long, I had to retake many courses to meet the university programs prerequisites. I also had to create a design portfolio, as my goal was to be a graphic designer. For my first year of general studies, I raised all my grades, developed a digital and traditional art portfolio, and applied to one of the top design programs in the country. Only 25 people got into the program every year. I thought that there was no way I was going to get in, but I also knew that if I didn't apply then I *definitely* wouldn't get in!

Surprisingly, I got accepted into the Visual Communications program and the start of my 4-year university journey began. Many people did not think it was possible I could raise 2 little boys, keep up with the extensive curriculum, keep food on our table and still graduate. This criticism provided me with more motivation to push through and succeed.

I had doubts along the way. I had to overcome my fear of failing, step out of my comfort zone, accept I was not perfect and leave all of my excuses at the door. For this also to work I had to defy all odds. I had to get my degree as a single mom, live off a $16,000 a year student loan, filter all negativity and just go for it!

To achieve great things and to move forward in your life, you need to learn to colour outside the lines and live outside the box. To take the unconventional road, dig deep and accept and truly believe that failure is not an option. Most of us have experienced a situation in our lives where you were asked to do something you really didn't want to do. The usual reply is, "Yeah, but...." This happens all the time. When someone asks you to work out, and you don't want to, you might say, "Yeah, but I'm not feeling good today." The next time she asks, you say "Yeah, but I have too much work to do today."

Eventually, this friend will stop asking you to work out with her because you just have too many excuses. She'll give up on you and you'll be stuck all by yourself. Excuses are another form of blaming something or someone for why you can't, won't, or just feel you shouldn't do. Excuses can be a way of avoiding the discomfort that comes from saying "no", or they can be a result of your insecurities and fears.

I call this "the but rule." I was super good at it, my whole life. I had excuses for everything: "the but rule" was the only reason why this book took me 2 years to get started. I had excuse after excuse until finally I just made it happen. "I'd love to write a book, but I don't think anyone would read it," I said. Or "Sure, I'll write my book, but right now I don't have the time." To finish this book, I had to eliminate all my "buts", sit down and focus on making it happen!

As a young teenager, I wanted to paint a wall in my house, which I labeled the feature wall. Every house should have a feature wall, which is a different colour than all the others and one that would stand out as an accent in their décor. My parents went along with it and said, "Great, we'll buy you the paint, if you paint the wall." I quickly agreed. What I didn't understand was that the wall needed more than one coat of paint: I had to prime it and then paint 2 coats of the soft green colour I chose.

The prime coat went on fine, but the wall seemed to get bigger as I was painting. The job was way more tiring than I ever thought. Halfway through the first coat, I quit. I was pooped, exhausted and found many other things to occupy my time with than finishing the wall. When my parents came home from work later that day, I was sitting in the back yard and they said, "Are you done for the day?" I replied, "No, I'm done for good, I need some help. It's too big of a wall for me." They reminded me of my promise to paint the wall. I told them it was too hard for me. My dad simply said, "You never finish anything you start, it's time you finish." My father's comment really resonated with me. I didn't want to disappoint him or my mom, so I finished painting the wall. Looking back, I remember how proud I felt after I finished. The wall looked great and although I didn't appreciate it at the time, I know my parents did the right thing by making me finish what I started.

You might think I would have learned from that experience, but I continued to use "the but rule" when I was training for squash. I would be running 400s, 800s, court sprints or drills and just stop. My coach, who was also my dad, would say "Let's go... you're half way there," and I would say "Yeah, but I'm shaky,", or "Yeah, but, I've got a stomach ache," or any other excuse I could come up with. Looking back, I am embarrassed how many times I used "the but rule" in my playing career. I was a really good player, and I still am today. But the fear of being great was always at the back of my mind.

What if I applied myself every day to every task and every exercise? What if I believed in myself and my capabilities without doubt? Maybe instead of settling for top 30 in the world I could have been top 15 or top 10 in the world. Instead my use of "the but rule" held me back, was my scapegoat, and my crutch so I could do what was only acceptable and not exceptional. What would happen if I just stopped using it?

We all live with our own version of "the but rule." Those are the excuses we use to simply do just enough to get by but not to push ourselves beyond where we are comfortable. It is our excuses that keep us where we are comfortable, where we remain colouring inside the lines, so we do not stand out or gain too much attention. If we stop coming up with excuses, maybe we would see some incredible results and achievements. To create a masterpiece, we need to colour outside of the lines. This is where the magic, the growth, and the records happen. Nothing exceptional happens when we play it safe, stay inside the box and fall back on our fear.

Our journey to happiness requires us to push beyond comfortable and safe. Happiness is discovered when we are challenged, strong and persistent, not when we are shadowed, weak and making excuses. In your journey to happiness it is important to remember to cut the excuses and just keep going for it. Be kind to yourself along the way and don't take yourself or those around you too seriously.

Here are 5 famous and very successful people who have achieved incredible things, who didn't use "the but rule" or make excuses:

1. J.K. Rowling was divorced, bankrupt and living on welfare when she wrote Harry Potter and The Philosopher's Stone. She was rejected by 12 publishers but didn't give up.

2. Michael Jordan was cut from his high school basketball team before becoming a basketball superstar. He was a 6-time NBA champion and was considered one of the best players in history.

3. Steven Spielberg applied 2 - 3 times to the University of Southern California and every time, he was rejected. As a child he had dyslexia, so he could not read or write properly. Today, he is now considered one of the founding filmmakers of the New Hollywood era.

4. Walt Disney was unwanted everywhere and nobody wanted to hire him. His studio was bankrupt. He was fired from his job because he wasn't creative enough. He is considered a pioneer of the American animation industry.

5. Oprah Winfrey was fired from her job as a television reporter because other people thought she was unfit for T.V. Today Oprah is one of America's media icons.

When you look at these incredible examples of commitment, determination and belief, there is no big mystery to it. In a nutshell, if you want something bad enough and decide that you will get it, then you will. Think back, you've done it before — you've lost the weight, gotten the job, bought the house, quit the nasty habit, gotten in shape, or asked someone out. If you've done it once, you can do it again!

CHAPTER SEVEN

STEP OUTSIDE YOUR COMFORT ZONE

> *"Move out of your comfort zone. You can only grow if you are willing to feel awkward and uncomfortable when you try something new."*
> ~ Brian Tracy ~

> *"To venture is to risk anxiety, but not to venture is to lose oneself. Security is elusive, to gain it you must risk it."*
> ~ Amanda Stark ~

The key to joy and happiness is to decide to go for your dreams, to stop listening to your old tired excuses, eliminate "the but rule," change your thinking, colour outside the lines and get on with it. Procrastination is the biggest stressor and it can linger for years.

Writing this book has always been a dream of mine. Two years ago, my business coach suggested that I should write a book. Unfortunately, I was held back by my own fears and insecurities. Fear of success, failure, overcoming my own self-doubt and of achieving my goal. What do I have to share? Who would want to read my story? It wasn't until I was diagnosed with depression and was at my lowest did I realize the only way out of my darkness was to help others get out of theirs. I realized I do have a story, which is worth sharing. My life experiences have made me who I am, proud, a survivor and an advocate of women's well-being and happiness. This book and any others I write will not be to just share my stories, but also to help and support others in their journey to a fulfilled life.

If you are thinking about doing something in your life, including deciding to be happy, my word of advice to you is to stop thinking, step outside your comfort zone and take action! One reason why we might be fearful of making a move or a change in our life is we are comfortable. You may have been in the same job, the same relationship, have been the same weight or lived in the same community for years. Maybe you have been happy, or at least thought you were happy, but something deep inside you is not feeling content and desires a change.

My youngest son is the perfect example of someone who does not settle to be inside his comfort zone. Straight out of high school he did not know what he wanted to do, so he took a full-time job as a mechanic. It paid very good money, he worked with his brother, he learned how to fix cars, and the dealership really liked him. Sounds good doesn't it?

It would have been, except deep down he was not happy. For him, working on cars was a hobby, and after 3 years, he discovered, it was not his passion. What he was passionate about was sports and working with children. So, he took a huge step outside his comfort zone, left his well-paying job and started a 6-year university program to become a teacher. He was scared of making the transition, as he knew how much university cost. He would have to cut back on many lifestyle perks, but he'd rather make that sacrifice now than live with regret later.

In the past, people were taught to work hard, get a good job, buy a house, get married, have a couple of children and be happy. You just work through your problems, live the life society expects of you, and don't question it. But what if you are not happy? What if there is a recession and you get laid off, what if your spouse is unfaithful, what if you can't have children? Are you simply supposed to accept this and be happy? You can stay in your comfort zone, or you can decide to colour outside the lines, get outside your comfort zone and find your Happiness Rescue.

Many people want to remain safe and secure. But what if you aren't fulfilled? What if you long for more stimulation or personal growth in your life? Inside your comfort zone, you may feel safe, but often times being in your comfort zone is the same as being complacent. You may be comfortable, but you are not happy.

We can't grow while we are safe. Whether it is a new relationship, starting a new job or business, getting a new pet, starting a family, buying a new house, standing up to a friend or family member, do whatever it is you will need to do. Step up and outside of your comfort zone to see change happen and to get what you desire.

Here are 7 benefits to stepping outside your comfort zone and towards your happiness rescue:

1. You have the opportunity to grow: you challenge yourself further by learning new skills and lessons, which will help you throughout your life.

2. You will learn more about yourself: taking risks will help you grow and teach you about your strengths, weaknesses, interests, passions, talents and skills. Each time you accomplish something new you become more confident, knowledgeable, proud and happy.

3. You expand yourself and your creativity: when you step outside your comfort zone and try something new you may discover a new hobby or talent you did not know you had. This is very exciting and rewarding!

4. You will increase your self-confidence: each time you accomplish or take on a new task, skill, event or situation you push yourself outside of your natural boundaries or limiting beliefs and build self-esteem. Insecurity loves to feed on your habit of not trying, so if you stop thinking and just do it, you will understand what is possible.

5. You will learn to deal with challenges: our lives are full of unpredictable and often spontaneous events and obstacles, which we need to step up and face. Knowing you have overcome and conquered them will build your confidence and be able to deal with bigger and bigger challenges throughout your life.

6. Your life will become cheerful: when you stop living the same day over and over like it was Groundhog Day, life will become more interesting and worth living. Risks will look like adventures and obstacles may look like opportunities. When you feel happier on the inside, your whole world will open up.

7. You will build new relationships: when you step outside your comfort zone, you will become more open to meeting all sorts of people you may not have met otherwise. To have good relationships with others, you must have a good relationship with yourself. Stepping outside your comfort zone, discovering who you are, and overcoming your fears will ultimately increase your overall happiness in your life.

Writing this book to you now, I will confess, I am completely out of my comfort zone. With each chapter, page, and word I am getting over my fear of failing, self-doubt, limiting beliefs, and insecurities. In a year, I know that I will look back and be proud of myself for accomplishing my goal. Happiness is about taking daily action, step by step, so you can begin to change your future and your life. Remember, for us to experience change and for change to actually occur we must step away outside of our comfort zone and colour outside the lines.

 I know how hard it can be to make the decision to change your life, so I have a special gift for you. In an eBook I wrote, I talk about everyday happiness and other areas you can consider when creating your own happiness rescue. Simply go to my website at <u>amandamaystark.com</u> find the yellow happy face book cover titled "Everyday Happiness - Unlock the Happiness You Deserve," fill in your information and download it right to your computer.

CHAPTER EIGHT

GET OUT OF YOUR RUT

"When you feel stuck and can't seem to move ahead, always remember that you don't have to get it right, you just have to get it going!"
~ Barbara Corcoran ~

"Edison failed 10,000 times before he made the electric light. Do not be discouraged if you fail a few times."
~ Napoleon Hill ~

In both my life and entrepreneurial journey, I have experienced many ups and downs. I've had to recover from injuries, break-ups, bankruptcy, re-marriage, unemployment, and mental illness. In my entrepreneurial venture, I was learning new skills, getting my life coaching certification, attracting clients, understanding online marketing, and adapting to new technology and software.

To get out of my own way, I had to believe in myself and accept and adapt to all the changes happening around me.

On the road to getting unstuck, we go through many different emotions and internal conflicts that create resistance. For some people this resistance is too much, and they end up quitting. For others, it adds fuel to the fire and they get more determined to succeed.

What do I mean by being stuck? In essence, being stuck is the feeling of being trapped by something, someone, your environment, or your life. It's like being stuck in quicksand, and the more you fight it, the further you sink. You get stuck when you think you should be something you're not or when you think life should be different than it is.

Being stuck results in a feeling of helplessness and frustration. For example, say you have been on a fitness program for a few months now and you are not seeing any results. You have no idea what to change in your program. You feel very frustrated because you don't know how to modify your training to get the results you want, so you feel stuck in the situation. So, do you reach out to someone or do you quit?

When I was laid off I had no idea what to do or where to turn. I applied to many jobs for months, but with the recession it seemed there were no jobs to be had. Feeling very stuck, frustrated, and angry, I just gave into it and stopped applying for jobs. After a few weeks of not focusing all my attention on it and taking a few online coaching courses, my intention became clear and I started up my own business.

Focusing so intently on a problem just magnifies it even more. We become frozen in negativity and begin to resent and neglect forward thinking action. If we allow the problem time to breathe and redirect our attention to other things, our initial problem either goes away or we figure out a way to solve it, and we can become unstuck.

Getting unstuck isn't easy. There are a few factors, which may get in your way of being unstuck. But these are in your hands to control if you are aware and handle them with a proactive approach. Feeling stuck is like being in a brain-storming meeting with colleagues, and your team comes up with a few creative suggestions. But one person, who doesn't contribute any solutions of their own, just comes up with excuses for why each idea won't work. Immediately, all the creative energy gets sapped out of the room, and you may as well end the meeting. When you're stuck, your brain is like that one unhelpful, negative person. Each time you come up with a potential solution, your mind just comes up with reasons why it won't work.

As an entrepreneur, I enjoy working on my own business. All the ideas and suggestions I have don't get dismissed. Instead, I save them for times when I do get stuck. If I were to have the "I've tried that before" attitude in my business, I may as well pack it in and go start collecting an employee paycheque again.

I find it incredibly frustrating when pessimistic colleagues surround me. Most great masterpieces are started and created from ideas and thoughts that are not necessarily unique, but simply represented with a new approach or new variable in place. These variables could be technology, budget, planning, environment, or even people.

Many times, "old" ideas, which did not work in the past, were not planned, prepared, marketed, or executed properly, so it's not surprising that they failed. When Thomas Edison invented the lightbulb, he kept trying different ways, different materials, and different formulas until he finally did it. If he had said, "Yeah, but we've tried that before and it didn't work," he wouldn't be known today as the inventor of the lightbulb. Instead someone else would have come across the same idea and invented it themselves, someone with a more positive, optimistic, open-minded attitude.

If you feel you are holding yourself back from trying something you have tried before in your past, but the desire to still do it is very much alive with you... go for it! This is the first step to recognizing you are stuck, and it is time to take forward action to becoming unstuck.

Maybe you'll be out for a walk through the park one day and you get the desire to do a cartwheel. You might think to yourself, "Well, I haven't done that since I was a kid," so you don't do it. Why does it matter that you haven't done it since you were a kid? Just do it! What would happen if you did the worst cartwheel ever? Could you embarrass yourself if someone is looking? If you're afraid of injuring yourself, find a soft, grassy area, then do it! You might embarrass yourself, or maybe you would just feel really proud of yourself that you stepped up and did a flippin' cartwheel! Next time you're at the park, try it and see what happens. Note how you feel!

A few weeks ago, my husband and I were out for our walk with our dogs. The day before I thought about doing a cartwheel, which I hadn't thought about doing for years! I suppressed my inclination to revisit my childhood days and carried on as normal. The next day out on our walk again, for a weird reason the thought came back to me and I said… screw it! I went for it and although my accuracy, form, and landing were far from perfect, all I remember is how incredibly freeing it was to let my adult body do a "kid thing," even if it was a simple cartwheel. My husband and I laughed and then guess what? Yep, I challenged him. There we were, in the park freely doing cartwheels. I'm sure our dogs thought we were crazy, but I bet that if they could do cartwheels, they too would have joined in the fun!

So, the next time you are in a meeting, in the park, at your house or wherever and you get an idea or notion to do something — just do it. Eliminate the statement "Yeah, but we've tried that before." Once again, you're using "the but rule" as an excuse. And just because you tried it before doesn't mean that you won't succeed this time!

Many people remain stuck in their lives because they are always "trying" things and not "doing" things. The emphasis is in the present action, not in the neutral phase and results do not happen if we are neutral, we do not get anywhere.

Here are 5 "Doing Things" you can put into action the next time you want to get unstuck from your rut:

1. Stop overthinking: just do it!
2. Face your fears: are you afraid to hurt yourself if you try a cartwheel? Find a soft grassy spot where you won't hurt yourself if you mess up the landing, and you'll be fine!
3. Break your routine and try something new!
4. Embrace change, one step at a time.
5. Be honest with yourself.

CHAPTER NINE

CONFRONT THE ESCAPE ARTIST

> *"The process of becoming unstuck requires tremendous bravery, because basically we are completely changing our way of perceiving reality."*
> ~ Pema Chodron ~

> *"True self-care is not salt baths and chocolate cake, it is making the choice to build a life you don't need to regularly escape from."*
> ~ Brianna Wiest ~

Being stuck can be debilitating. If we don't take action, we'll never get out of our rut. We can find ourselves overthinking, feeling depressed or escaping our life. You might feel afraid to move and hide from all new experiences, relationships and ultimately stop growing as a person. When we begin to hide from our lives we begin to close ourselves off and look for excuses if we are asked to do something or go somewhere. We seek to escape from our own realities, because we have limited our own happiness and growth as a person.

When we feel the need to escape, we are emotionally stuck. In our minds there is a chance of rejection or failure, so we turn to an escape plan or avoidance tactics to protect us. This is an internal coping mechanism, which has been conditioned to respond to any immediate threats that come up. We could be avoiding certain situations, painful experiences from the past, or new experiences we are being asked to do, so internally we retract and escape from it.

To a certain extent everyone avoids issues they regularly experience. It is quite natural if the house needs cleaning, we often do all we can to avoid doing it and instead escape to Facebook, watch a movie, or head out to our garden. We avoid things we feel are painful, uncomfortable, or we simply do not feel like doing. Unfortunately, this leads to a habit of procrastination, which can begin to snowball and become a huge stressor in our lives.

Since I was laid off of my job I have experienced many cases of escaping from my reality. I avoided going somewhere where I knew other people would go. I knew they would ask me how I'm doing and how my new business is going. What do I say? Do I tell the truth and tell them how much I'm struggling? Or do I lie and say, "Yeah, I am awesome, and my new business is going great, I've got tons of clients and I'm so happy I got laid off!"

Distorting the truth, though helpful in the moment, ultimately will not lead to any favourable outcome. When we are avoiding we are stuck in a constant maze of doubt, uncertainty, fear, and self-loathing. We are running away from these things as a survival technique, but avoidance does not help our self-esteem, confidence or overall happiness.

Escapism isn't necessarily a bad thing, especially when used in moderation. Think of escapism as neither good nor bad, and instead like sugar or salt. You can sprinkle it on top of your life to make it better, but too much will ruin the whole thing. Avoiding reality can cause problems at work, damage personal relationships and your productivity can plummet.

Today, social media is a tool that many people use to escape. Whether it is Facebook, Instagram, Twitter, Snapchat, or YouTube, these platforms can be a massive escape tool or crutch in everyone's lives. When my children were young, we decided to put a basket on the back shelf. When it was dinnertime, the phones had to go into the basket. This was also a rule for our kid's friends who would come over too. One time, there were about 3 or 4 young boys sitting up at our breakfast bar waiting for my husband to cook them lunch and he turned around and all of them had their heads down. He said, "What are you guys doing? Praying or texting each other? Phones in the basket please."

Escapism on our phones and our computers is so easy to do, and we avoid any form of direct social interaction with anyone. Just pay attention the next time you are waiting in your doctor's or dentist's office and see how many people are on their phones and how many are reading "old fashioned" books? I'd be one of the people reading a book! Furthermore, many people are on their phones while walking, and do not even look up to say hello, or to make sure they are not going to bump into anything.

Some escape strategies you may be guilty of in your own life could be:

- Isolating yourself
- Being defensive
- Addictive behaviours (alcohol, over eating, drugs etc.)
- Blaming and/or complaining
- Criticizing others
- Avoiding meeting new people
- Avoiding responsibilities
- Sabotaging yourself or others
- Excessive worrying
- Comparing yourself to others

There are several tactics we use to keep ourselves comfortable and to avoid what we do not want to deal with. You might procrastinate and put things off or distract yourself with other tasks to avoid the things that require your attention. Escapism is a means of sabotage. We can only get better through seeking ways to wean ourselves, to get unstuck and move forward.

Here are 5 tactics you can use if you find yourself escaping your reality, wasting time or putting off what needs to be done:

1. Avoid distractions
   Put away your phone, iPad and get away from social media.

2. Use a timer to manage your time
   Try the Pomodoro Technique that uses a timer to break down work into intervals. Traditionally 25 minutes of work, then you enjoy a 5-minute break. This has really helped me writing this book. The technique teaches you to work with time, instead of struggling against it.

3. Avoid distorting the truth
   This only enables our escapism and delays positive emotions of success and happiness.

4. Journal about what you're avoiding
   If you find you are escaping your daily tasks or repeatedly avoiding certain things, start writing about them. Why are you are feeling the way you are? How does avoiding these things help you in the long run? What can you choose differently which might create a more favourable outcome?

5. Ask for help
   My husband has always been excellent for this, as he has become my accountability partner. I have opened up to him enough that he knows my triggers. We have a code word we use when we are out, which if he notices I am avoiding or escaping a certain situation or person he will say the word, which signifies to me a decision to either change my action or ignore. As we practice this more and more, I am finding ways to act

and overcome my desire for avoidance, which is helping me, overcome this behaviour.

CHAPTER TEN

JUST QUIT PROCRASTINATING

*"A year from now you may wish
you had started today."*
~ Karen Lamb ~

*"Procrastination is one of the most common
and deadliest of diseases and its toll on
success and happiness is heavy."*
~ Wayne Gretzky ~

Procrastination is the biggest stress over, which we have absolute control. We can procrastinate in every facet of our life. This can keep us stuck in a rut. Like escapism, procrastination is a way which we avoid doing things that should be done, and can become a factor in our overall life happiness.

From the simplest task of making a phone call, paying your bills, going to the grocery store, finishing painting the living room wall, walking the dog, or getting out of bed, procrastination can be the difference between your life moving forward in a happy direction or standing still and not moving at all.

There's a big difference between procrastinating and taking a break or resting. For me, we all need to rest and to forgive ourselves for the conscious decision to take a break. Going back to my sports training days, on Sundays, when I did not have a tournament or event, I would allow myself to sleep in, have pancakes at noon and hang out in my pyjamas all day. I needed the one day off a week for my muscles, mind and energy to reboot and rest, so they could fire back up for the next week of training. Taking a rest day reduced the risk of burnout, fatigue and injury, which extended my season and increased my results.

Even now, writing this book, I commit to writing 6 days a week anywhere between 1500 - 2000 words per day. If I do that, then I allow myself to take Sundays off. On Sundays, I do research, chill, sleep, hang-out in my garden, or binge-watch Netflix. I don't feel guilty because I have accomplished my goals for the week.

Procrastinating, on the other hand, is much different than taking a conscious break. Procrastination comes with lingering feelings like guilt and being overwhelmed, which can lead to self-blame and negative self-talk. Procrastinate long enough, and you might feel so stressed out you lose sleep, feel depressed, and worry all the time. If we continue to procrastinate, our goals will never be met, we will feel constantly discouraged and end up quitting before we've even given ourselves a chance. As an athlete, if I were to procrastinate my in daily training, I would never have reached the elite level I did, and as a writer, if I were to procrastinate I would never have written this book.

One of my clients was struggling with procrastination in her life. She kept telling me how much she had to do, and she had no idea where to start, so she didn't. Instead, she kept spinning her wheels and stressing about how busy she was. I said to her "What is the most important thing you have to do today?" She then began to recite everything she had to do, without actually answering my question. The list included; going to the grocery store, doing laundry, packing for her trip she was going on (in 3 days), working on a presentation, cooking dinner, booking her kids appointments and the list kept going on.

I felt panic and overwhelm in her voice and she was pacing as she spoke. I asked her to sit down, relax, and breathe. To feel the pressure come off her chest, to lower her eyes and decompress. After a few moments, I asked her the same question, "What is the most important thing you have to do today?" She replied, "Working on my presentation because it is due tomorrow." She suddenly realized, everything else on her to-do list really wasn't important. It was her presentation, which was the catalyst of avoiding and adding everything else on the list to avoid doing what was important.

The grocery shopping, cooking dinner, booking appointments and packing for a trip, which wasn't for another 3 days, could wait. She could order take-out and all the other items could be done after she had finished her presentation.

If you notice yourself procrastinating, here are some helpful remedies, which you can implement into your life immediately.

1. Ask yourself, what is the most important thing you have to get done today? If you focus on the most important thing, you will find your stress will be drastically reduced. The most important thing is usually the thing about which you are procrastinating and is the root of the panic, anxiety and pressure.

2. Get yourself a calendar. That could be a digital calendar in your phone or on your computer or, for the tactile person, the "old-school" calendar on your desk.

3. Bite off only what you can chew. One of the triggers for someone to procrastinate is when they have too much to do.

4. Just do it. If you're procrastinating, pick a task that you're avoiding and just get it done!

5. Celebrate! Just as important as it is to accomplish tasks and to reach goals, it is just as important to celebrate your successes when you do achieve them.

CHAPTER ELEVEN

A Self-Empowered Mindset

"It isn't what you have, or who you are, or what you are doing that makes you happy or unhappy, it is what you think about."
~ Dale Carnegie ~

"Self-esteem is the relationship you have with yourself, your relationship with other people, and how you feel in the company of others. Do you see yourself as a person who adds great value to the lives of others? Or do you feel unimportant, as if your opinion doesn't matter?"
~ Scott Allan ~

Oftentimes, we have self-defeating habits that can get in the way of happiness. Changing these habits requires changing your mindset. The way in which we go from self-defeating to self-empowering ourselves is critical in our work, relationships, finances, health and overall happiness.

People who know me may be surprised at what they read in this book. Others often perceive me as confident, strong, and successful. But that couldn't be further from the truth. I carried so much self-doubt with me every day. Most people didn't know the real me. From athlete, to single mom, to corporate life, to layoff, to building my business through all these stages in my life I had very little confidence in myself, but one thing I did have was determination.

Once, when I was travelling to the national championships, my friend and I were discussing our goals. I asked him: "Are you ever afraid that you're just going to miss the ball and you'll be horrible, lose, and everyone will laugh at you?" His response stunned me. "Absolutely never," he said. "I know I have put in the work and I'm confident when I walk on the court." The idea that someone could really believe that strongly in themselves was profound.

Looking back, I began to realize why I was never really happy when I played. I was always struggling with my self-esteem and it was exhausting. How did I look on the court? What was I wearing? What were people thinking when they were watching me? How could I make my parents proud of me? I was coping with all of this, while trying to perform at my best. These demons I carried around made my task of an athlete ten times harder than just believing in myself, walking on the court and kicking my opponent's ass.

Self-esteem refers to the way you value yourself. If you think that you aren't worthy of good things, or that you'll never be good enough, you have low self-esteem. Someone with a healthy level of self-esteem is confident in their abilities. When you have low self-esteem, you end up getting in your own way, and preventing yourself from being happy because you believe that you don't deserve to be happy.

The root of your self-esteem is your feeling of worth and how capable and likeable you believe yourself to be. Being capable means you can make things happen and get things done. Likeable people are people that other people enjoy having around. Therefore, the more you see yourself as capable and likeable, the more valuable you estimate yourself to be, and the higher your self-esteem.

If you do not see yourself as capable or likeable, then you have low self-esteem. You never see yourself as good enough for anything. You may feel like you are beneath everyone and no matter how hard you try you will never match up to others. You constantly compare yourself to others and think that they look better, have more, or are more talented.

Self-esteem refers to whether *you* think of yourself as capable and likeable. Your friends may like you, and your boss and coworkers may see you as quite capable. But if you don't see *yourself* that way, then you have low self-esteem. Having low self-esteem does *not* mean that you are not worthy of good things, or less deserving than others. It's a reflection of your beliefs.

Some symptoms of believing you are not good enough are:

- Jealousy
- Fear of Criticism
- Pessimism
- Trouble saying "no"
- Lack of Confidence
- Fear of taking risks
- Depression
- Insecurity
- Need for acceptance and approval
- Avoiding eye contact
- Perfectionism
- Fear of taking action
- Resentment
- Difficulty trusting people

At the root of low self-esteem is the feeling of self-doubt. As a negative belief, self-doubt takes away your feeling of certainty about you. It is the waterfall, which begins to take over all your thoughts and feelings, crowding the positive thoughts. If you are not feeling capable or likeable, then you are not feeling valued and then your self-doubt just compounds itself.

Low self-esteem and self-doubt can hold you back from accomplishing what it is you really want in your life. You could have everything you need for a successful business, but if you do not believe in yourself at your inner core, then you may as well have nothing. If you are looking for an incredible partner, a new job, to get your degree, to write a book, or to play a new instrument, you must first believe in yourself to attract what it is you want.

One time, I became involved with a man who I thought was incredible. He was kind, adventurous and at the beginning treated me like a queen. He knew I was a single mom, but after I introduced him to my sons, he became a jerk. I had a feeling that he wasn't just seeing me and that he may have been dating someone else too. When I asked him about it, he lied to my face and denied it. I had low self-esteem at the time, so I accepted his answer — over and over again.

When I told a friend about my suspicions and insecurities of the relationship, she gave me some great advice. This man had become verbally and mentally abusive, but I tolerated it. He was handsome and very popular in the community, and I was struggling with low self-esteem. My friend said, "Amanda, until you learn to become your own princess you will never be treated like one." WOW! She was right, unless I started to believe in myself, what I was worth and the value of what I bring to a relationship, this guy and all guys to follow would continue to treat me poorly.

I broke up with him and applied to the university, which I talked about in chapter 6. I could have held myself back by believing that I was not good enough. I was a mature student; why would the program accept me? But I didn't. Instead I put together my portfolio, sent it in with my transcript and was accepted! I packed up my 2 sons, moved closer to family, attended and graduated from one of the top visual communication universities in the country — all because I decided to become my own princess.

The pressure we create on ourselves to fit in, to be accepted, and to be perfect can be overwhelming. The stress alone can cause more problems to your relationships, your health and your happiness. We will never be able to be the way everyone else wants us to be because we are independent people with unique qualities, wants and desires.

Happiness comes from having a positive, confident and healthy self-esteem. Part of developing healthy self-esteem is making a commitment to yourself and not trying to please the world. Rather than chasing temporary emotional rewards by playing games with the truth, you can learn to stand up for what you believe, speak the truth in love, live through stormy times with energy and joy, and little by little rewrite your life script.

If you are struggling to feel happy with yourself and lacking self-esteem and confidence here are 5 ways you too can begin to eliminate your self-doubt:

1. <u>Mirror work</u>
   Look in the mirror every morning and every evening and tell yourself you are beautiful. This may sound corny to begin with but trust me…it works!

2. Accept your flaws
   Who cares if you're not a supermodel! Love yourself the way you are, and others will too.

3. Stay positive
   Surround yourself with positive, fun people. Spend time with optimists and others who do not blame or complain. Stay away from those who love the drama and who are overly critical. It is amazing how much your self-esteem will skyrocket!

4. Avoid following the followers
   Stand up for who you are and what you believe in. You and others will respect you more for trusting your own values and instincts than entrusting and following others.

5. Live in the now
   Accept the past is gone and the present is your now. To be emotionally healthy you must move from victim to victor. The strong person with a confident self-esteem is one who refuses to let the past control what happens today.

CHAPTER TWELVE

WIPING OUT LIMITING BELIEFS

"Don't limit yourself. Many people limit themselves to what they think they can do. You can go as far as your mind lets you. What you believe, remember, you can achieve."
~ Mary Kay Ash ~

"Do the uncomfortable. Become comfortable with these acts. Prove to yourself that your limiting beliefs die a quick death if you will simply do what you feel uncomfortable doing."
~ Darren Rowse ~

Limiting beliefs are the don'ts, the cant's, the shouldn'ts, and the wouldn'ts, which you tell yourself. They are the underlining excuses or justification for your actions. They hold us back just by our belief in them! There are no limits to what you can achieve in your life other than the limits you put on yourself!

Limited thinking paralyzes you from the start. You become so obsessed and distracted by making excuses and convincing yourself you can't do something that you don't even give yourself the opportunity to try. This way of thinking is the biggest preventer to achieving your goals and ultimately your happiness.

Beliefs are conditioned perceptions that are built upon old memories of pain and pleasure. These memories are based on how we have interpreted and emotionalized our experiences over time. By attaching ourselves emotionally to people, events, and circumstances, we effectively build the foundations of our belief systems. These belief systems, therefore, are nothing more than patterns of experience, which have created our mindset and perception of our reality.

Beliefs are essentially assumptions we make about ourselves, about others, and about how we expect things to be in our world. We all have theories, ideas, and explanations about how things are and how they ought to be. Likewise, we make all these conclusions about life and about other people, all of which help us make better sense of the world. Beliefs are anchors that help express our understanding of the world around us.

You've probably had self-limited beliefs at some time. Perhaps you thought that you weren't good enough, that you don't deserve success, that you couldn't afford that car or lose ten pounds. Over time, these thoughts you create in your mind become imprinted in your belief system and no matter what you do, you will never be able to get over them unless you change your thinking.

I was working with a client recently, Maggie (not her real name), who was having some challenges at her job and with her team at work. She had a decent paying job as a Coordinator, was good at what she did, but after a few years in the same position she was getting a bit bored and was looking for a change. At her annual review she had asked her boss for a promotion many times, and every year her boss just kept telling her she was working on it. Over time, Maggie became more hesitant to ask for the promotion, so she settled with the fact that she had a good job. Deep down she was not happy, but because she told herself that she didn't deserve the promotion and that there was no point in asking for what she wanted, she wasn't doing anything to change her situation.

Maggie gave up and let her boss have all the power. She continued to fall into her limiting belief system. After a few weeks of working through the SMILE for Women program, we went through a step-by-step process to clearing all Maggie's limiting beliefs. Although Maggie could not control her boss, she could control her beliefs and reactions to the situation. Maggie decided she was worth more than her boss was crediting her for, so she started to look around for other better paying, more challenging positions. Within a month, she accepted a Director position with a new company and finally got the recognition, pay, confidence, and happiness she was seeking.

In any situation or experience, we are controlled by our thoughts. The average person has between 50,000 and 70,000 thoughts per day! What happens to these thoughts when they come into our brains? What do they create?

In the book "Secrets of the Millionaire Mind," T. Harv Eker introduces a formula of how you can create your reality when it comes to wealth. But this formula can also help us create our Happiness Rescue. The "Process of Manifestation" goes like this: Thoughts → Feelings → Actions = Results. Your thoughts lead to your feelings, which lead to your actions and generate your results. So, if you have limiting beliefs or thoughts, they are going to create limiting or negative feelings, which will inhibit your actions and therefore impede your results.

Over the past couple of years throughout my entrepreneurial journey, through my failures, false hopes, wasted money, self-defeat, health challenges and all the other water which has gone under the bridge, it was at my son's wedding where I suddenly recognized my true worth. Here I was sitting at this beautiful ceremony with my son marrying the love of his life, the clouds parted, and the sun appeared. Suddenly I believed I could do anything I put my mind to. If I could only keep the emotion of that day close to my heart, how happy, peaceful and proud I felt, and draw from that positive energy, I could accomplish anything!

Remember how my business coach suggested that I write a book? At first, I dismissed the idea. But the week after the wedding, I started this book. I didn't know where to start; I just started writing. The next day I got up and started writing again, and so on and so forth. I thought that I could help people get unstuck, reach their goals, and build confidence. These thoughts led to my feelings of value, service and community. Based on those feelings, I took action and wrote every day to ultimately have the result of writing my Happiness Rescue book.

If you are feeling controlled and restricted by your limiting beliefs there are 5 ways, which you can begin to recognize, redirect, and redesign your limited thinking:

1. Recognize your limiting beliefs
   Think back to an experience you have had where you would have preferred a different outcome. What thoughts were going through your head, how did you feel about yourself, what outcome would you have chosen differently? Write down any limiting beliefs that come up. This may be an emotional experience, but one worth venturing.

2. Question your limiting beliefs
   Once you have a list of beliefs take this time now to challenge them. Why are they false? Moving forward why do you choose to change them? What negative effects have they had on you? What reasons do you have to not believe they are true?

3. Choosing to change or hang on to them
   What are the consequences of continuing to live by these beliefs? In 6 months, if you continue to accept this limiting belief as the truth, where will you be? Is this acceptable to you? Are you willing to get

uncomfortable and make some mistakes to change this belief?

4. Create new powerful beliefs
   Now we get into the transformation part of the process where we take the belief or beliefs we are choosing to change and create new more passionate beliefs to move forward with. For me, this was to change "I hate writing" to "I do not have to be a perfect writer. Just write."

5. Practice, practice, practice.
   New patterns and belief systems do not happen overnight. Just like with any new skill, they will change slowly but surely with repetition, acknowledgement and awareness. So, when you feel yourself going down the negative belief trap, catch yourself (snap an elastic, tap yourself on the leg, or give yourself a mental brain knock), and repeat your new positive, powerful belief.

CHAPTER THIRTEEN

THE COMPARISON TRAP

"The only limits you have are the limits you believe."
~ Wayne Dyer ~

"You do not determine your success by comparing yourself to others, rather you determine your success by comparing your accomplishments to your capabilities."
~ Zig Ziglar ~

What has your life been like up until now? Have you been like my friend who feels like they can just overcome anything, and knows that he will accomplish his goals? Or do you struggle with comparing yourself to others and questioning whether you are good enough?

If you are like most people, you probably do compare yourself to others, or have in the past. I am guilty of this all the time! I will say to my husband on one of our dog walks when we see another woman coming our way, "Do I look as good as her? Am I her size?" But these questions just put him in a no-win situation with his response. If he says, "Yes, honey, you look great," then I wonder if he's just saying that to make me feel better, or if he really means it. Yet, after 12 years of marriage, I must admit that he is a massive reason why I still have any confidence at all.

Isn't that sad? Do I honestly need my husband to validate if I am good enough? Depression is like a roller coaster ride, and this one is tricky. Depression can play with your mind, one day you'll feel great and then the next day you feel like you cannot do anything, but what we must do is to prompt reminders for ourselves and not let our surroundings be triggers for us.

We need to remember that we are not our mind. We are also not the thoughts we play out in our mind. When we compare ourselves to others, we are downgrading our own selves and criticizing our self-worth. It does not matter in any situation, at any age. If we are constantly telling ourselves we are not good enough, we will believe this indefinitely, unless we develop coping skills to change this behaviour.

I was very good at my sport. I would never have played for my country in 5 world championships if I wasn't, but first I had to believe in myself. The way I handled this was I would visualize myself in different situations, different environments, playing different people and picture various outcomes and how I would feel. If I was super nervous in a warm-up, or if I was playing a really strong opponent, I would transition my thoughts into action and hit each shot with the intention of making my opponent feel less confident. This sounds easy, but it was a tactic, which took years to execute because first I had to recognize how I was feeling.

Most of our inner conversations or unhappiness originates from our feelings. Remember our feelings are generated from our thoughts. So, by this theory if we can recognize when we have self-defeating thoughts, give ourselves a sign, change our reaction to our thoughts we can divert our feelings to more favourable outcomes.

In most cases, the funny thing is those people who we are comparing ourselves to are most likely comparing themselves to us. It is a vicious cycle, which does not go away. We need to be aware and practice how to triumph over our thoughts when they are not working in our favour. A thought like "I'm not good enough" is negative self-talk. If we talk to ourselves like this, we become that school-yard bully. But instead of it being some other kid, we are beating our own selves up. This is one of the worst kinds of bullying because it is self-inflicted.

I have had clients who have physically hurt themselves dealing with anxiety, depression, or other forms of mental illness. This type of self-abuse — their actions — was a result of their feelings, which came from their thoughts. When we verbally abuse ourselves and create negative inner chaos inside, this is just as dangerous and may lead to physical self-harm.

Battling your inner bully with constant conflicting arguments and fights inside your mind is tough! If you are verbally cutting yourself down, please open up to someone, whether that be a partner, doctor, therapist, life coach or friend. You do not need to create your own drama or defeat yourself. You can flip the switch and become your own best advocate, so you can turn your thoughts into positive feelings, actions and a happier life!

If you struggle with negative self-talk, one exercise you can do is mirroring. It may feel a little strange to begin with. Once you do it a few times, you will begin to see the benefits. What you do is stand in front of the mirror and say positive thoughts to counter your negative self-talk. If one of the things you say to yourself is "I'm not good enough," then you look in the mirror and say, "I am good enough" or "I am proud of myself." If you worry too much about what others think say, "I do not care what others think." You're reinforcing the idea that you are more than everything you are telling yourself.

Furthermore, here are 7 things I can offer you to remember when you are tempted to be mean to yourself:

1. It is not just you
   The people you compare yourself to, also compare themselves to other people. We all compare ourselves to other people. Remember that those people are also comparing themselves to you! Stop it and remember what a great person you truly are.

2. Your mind can lie to you
   "Don't believe everything you think. Thoughts are just that — thoughts." This quote by Allan Lokos reminds us that we are not our thoughts, so stop believing everything you think.

3. There is more right with you than wrong with you
   According to Jon Kabat-Zinn, "Until you stop breathing, there's more right with you than wrong with you." Get some perspective. It is very true, you are alive, so enjoy it!

4. Allow yourself love when you feel you deserve it the least
   While I was battling depression and feeling such lows from self-esteem, energy, belief in myself and had no idea who I was, my husband accepted me for who I was. He didn't try to hurry the process. He understands what I need when I ask him on our walks my insecure questions of my self-worth. He always has my back and is a reassuring confidant for me. It is vital for you to connect with someone when you are being your own inner bully.

5. Accept where you are in the moment
   You have to fully accept the now before you can move onto the future or what's next. You cannot move on to the next challenge or chapter until you can accept, acknowledge and appreciate who and where you are. Embrace, make peace and be kind with where you are, and your journey towards your future. Once you do,

receiving something new will be more rewarding and fulfilling, making you happier and more joyful.

6. Focus on progress not perfection
One of the biggest causes of self-loathing is the need to get it right. Many times, we strive for perfection over progression and in the meantime do nothing because we don't "get it right" the first time. When I decided to finally step up and write this book, I learned from my past and instead of going for perfection, every day I just went for my goal. I set up a schedule and regardless of how good the first draft was, it would never get done if I was constantly editing to make it perfect. So, I continued to write, every day. If you are holding back from doing something, take the action you need and stop waiting for all the stars to align. Take daily action, stop critiquing yourself and give yourself daily pats on the back for reaching your goal.

7. You can't hate your way into loving yourself
As I approach my 50th birthday, it is kind of sad to reflect and think how many years I really did not like myself. I would beat myself up with self-doubt, negative self-talk and insecurities to last a lifetime. It took being at my lowest with my "worst day" to realize it was wake up time. For all the time I hated or disliked myself I was regressing towards anything I could have which would ultimately have made me happy. Telling yourself you are a failure won't make you any more successful. Telling yourself you are worthless and unlovable won't make you feel any more worthy or loved.

I know it's not simple, but we do make it more complicated than it really is. The only way to stop your inner bully from playing havoc is to ignore him or her and shut him or her down before he or she opens his or her thoughts. You are enough just as you are and a little mental high-five or personal pat on the back will go a long way to loving yourself, being your own best friend and being happy!

CHAPTER FOURTEEN

SET YOUR GOAL AND ESTABLISH RITUALS

"The key to forming good habits is to make them part of your rituals. I have a morning ritual, afternoon ritual, and Sunday ritual. It's one way to bundle good habits into regular times that you set aside to prepare yourself for the life you want. Rituals help you form habits."
~ Lewis Howes ~

"You must define your why before you can begin with the what and the how."
~ Maria Reyes McDavis ~

At a very young age, I was always about setting goals. I was the provincial tennis champion at age 13, after playing tennis for 3 years. By sixteen, I won my first of 3 Canadian squash championships. Setting goals was key to my success. When I attended university, I was a financially strapped single mom, however I set new goals for myself each semester. I graduated in 4 years with a Bachelor of Design and a major in Visual Communications. Similarly, after I had children and had gained weight, I set weight loss and fitness goals, where I was back to my pre-pregnancy weight within 6 months of having both my boys. We humans are always searching for something and striving to reach another goal.

Our goals are not only defined by the one big goal, but they are achieved by setting mini goals. Leading up to the national championships, I had 6 other tournaments. For each tournament I had a goal, and each goal built upon the success of the last one. Meeting these goals led up to achieving the big goal — national champion!

Before entering the national or world championships I always set strategic goals. Instead of establishing outrageously high and unattainable expectations, I would set realistic yet challenging expectations. The challenge with setting unrealistic or high expectations, whether in your job, your relationships, your finances or your health, is you will feel very disappointed by the outcome or with yourself if you don't achieve the goal. The opposite of this is setting low or easy expectations as you will never truly challenge yourself, reach your fullest potential or accomplish your goals.

For example, you set yourself a goal of losing ten pounds. An unrealistic goal is for you to lose the ten pounds in one month. If you were to eat very little and exercise all the time, you would probably be left not feeling well, disappointed, and discouraged before you have lost even half the weight. If you were to set low expectations, you may also end up quitting because you may become less motivated, uninspired, and pessimistic about yourself and your results. So, what if you had a strong goal, vision, desire, enforced habits, rituals, a measurable and manageable plan with no expectations other than to take each day one by one? To give up control of the situation other than to focus on what you had to do today, not tomorrow or next week, but to take action on the task at hand and to let go of everything else.

Can you imagine how many goals you would reach taking this approach?

The first thing you really need to establish before setting a new goal is to ask yourself a few questions. Why do you want to accomplish this goal? Have you wanted this for a long time? Is now the time to make it a reality? Is the goal realistic and attainable? Can your goal be measured?

You may find the S.M.A.R.T acronym helpful when establishing your goals. S.M.A.R.T goals are clear and reachable. Broken down, they should be:

- **S**pecific (simple, sensible, significant)
- **M**easurable (meaningful, motivating)
- **A**chievable (agreed, attainable)
- **R**elevant (reasonable, realistic and resourced, results-based)
- **T**ime bound (time-based, time limited, time/cost limited, timely, time-sensitive)

It is vital you have a clear understanding of why you really want to attain a particular goal. Planning, implementing, and taking action every day to reach your goal will not be easy, however if you have defined your reason, the true essence of why you want to accomplish something, then understanding your why will give you the motivation to power through.

I knew I wanted to write a book; in fact, my life coach challenged me 2 years ago. My reason why, at the time, was not strong enough and I put this labour of love on hold. Then after attending my son's wedding, I felt such a strong epiphany of self-love that I could not deny my intentions. My "why" became very apparent to help myself recover, but to also help others overcome sadness and rescue their own happiness.

Establishing daily rituals is necessary to achieving your goals. To reach a particular goal, we need to enforce and consistently perform particular rituals into our daily life. Daily rituals provide the framework for doing the work necessary to achieve the micro goals. Over time, this work adds up to the larger goal. These rituals can determine success or failure.

Rituals are the consistent daily actions you take that help you build habits over time. Those habits then shape your thoughts, beliefs and emotions. You already partake in a multitude of daily rituals: brushing your teeth when you wake up, eating breakfast in the morning, and watching your favourite television show at the same time each week.

These are just 3 examples of the dozens of rituals you undoubtedly indulge in on a regular basis.

All these rituals power your day and they can either work for you or against you. If your goal is to lose ten pounds, but every night you sit down to watch your favourite reality show and eat a bag of chips, you probably won't lose the ten pounds. In my quest to write this book, I had to change my daily ritual of being on social media to only once a day for a maximum of fifteen minutes and commit to writing instead. We need to be aware of our rituals. Set your intentions and ask yourself if what you are doing is adding to or distracting from what you ultimately want.

One common goal is to live a happier, more fearless life. If you want to reach this goal, you must commit to your daily happiness rituals, such as meditation or journaling. If you can't commit, that may be why you are not feeling happy and still experiencing fear. You might experience fear of success, fear of commitment, or fear of being happy.

Goals do not make positive changes happen. Daily rituals do. Every day you wake up, you have the choice to execute or avoid your daily rituals. Depending on what you choose, you will move closer to or farther from your goal. As Mariel Hemingway said, "A daily ritual is a way of saying I'm voting for myself; I'm taking care of myself."

Are you having trouble committing to your daily rituals? Envision your success. What will it feel like to accomplish this goal? Writing this book is very important to me, because I want to know what it feels to be an author who has helped change lives. If I didn't feel like writing 1 day, I would asked myself "Do you want to still be sitting on this book this time next year? Can you imagine how you will feel when it is finished?" Envisioning my success motivates me to write at least 1600 words daily and commit to writing for 4 hours every day.

Consider this: you want to start your own online business so you can earn some passive income. Maybe you want to retire early, or maybe you want more vacation money. So, you set a goal: within 1 month, you will have a profitable online business. However, leading up to that all you do is talk about the idea of having an online business. You're not actually taking the action steps to get your business up and running. You could be creating a business plan, taking online courses, reaching out to online mentors and getting their ideas and feedback. These types of activities would not take up much of your day if you take daily action to complete them. But if you try to do it all the day before your deadline, you will just be stressed and wonder how anyone ever makes money online!

Does this sound familiar to you? Which areas of your life are you unhappy with? It is time to shift your focus away from your goal and more toward the rituals, which support them. Having daily rituals is one of the most powerful things you can do to help you change your life for the better.

To reach a new goal, you have to begin new rituals to make it happen. Sometimes, these new rituals may put you out of your comfort zone. You may start to overanalyze your decision. Pretty soon you are bashing yourself up mentally with negative self-talk, justifying why you shouldn't do it all because you are afraid to change. But the greatest successes and achievements come from when people step outside their comfort zones, colour outside the lines and just go for it. Begin with smaller rituals, and once you are more comfortable then advance the ritual or add a new one to your day.

Remember to keep focused on your vision, your reason why and take daily steps without self-doubt. My former husband, an Olympian badminton player, decided last year he was going to do a full Ironman and raise funds for the Calgary Mental Health Association. He has been personally affected by mental illness and knows how paralyzing it can be, to individuals and their families. A full Ironman consists of swimming 2.4 miles, biking 112 miles and running 26.22 miles. Our sons and close family members initially thought he was mad: he's now in his early 50's and has never swam, biked, or ran these kinds of distances ever! But that didn't stop him.

After several months of watching him prepare, we could not do anything other than get on the support wagon and cheer him on. He hired a coach to develop a workout plan to prepare himself. Every day he follows his plan: he is either in the pool, lake, on the bike or out for a run. He has aches and pains, but daily rituals help him achieve his goal. He's not just doing it for himself, but also to help others with mental illness.

The next time you want to lose ten pounds, whether it's for an upcoming wedding, reunion, or just because you don't feel great, get some help. Put a plan in place and take daily action. Not motivated to work out? Imagine how great you will feel when you lose the weight and put on that dazzling dress you want to fit into. You can do it if you believe in your vision and take daily action to make it happen.

Here are 5 steps you can take to begin to reach your goals:

1. Determine what you want to achieve
   This is easy. What is it you want? Start with the 1 thing you want to achieve in the next 12 months. If you are not sure, here are some suggested areas: Health, Wealth, Relationships, Happiness or Career.

2. Breakdown how you will achieve your goal
   This does not need to be complicated. You'll learn more about how to do this in the next chapter.

3. Write it down
   Write down your goal. Make it as specific as you can.

4. Make yourself accountable
   Use whatever works for you. You can envision your success, remind yourself of your commitment, or find a friend to share your daily wins with. Once you gain momentum, you will find that it gets easier to show up every day, and you will achieve your goal!

5. Take daily action, don't just wish for it
   Now you have a goal and a plan to accomplish it. You need to take daily action to make it happen. Wishing will not make it so. You must show up, be intentional, and commit to the process day by day.

CHAPTER FIFTEEN

THINK SMALL TO ACHIEVE BIG

"A dream written down with a date becomes a goal. A goal broken down into steps becomes a plan. A plan backed by action makes your dreams come true."
~ Greg Reid ~

"It's not about perfect. It's about effort. And when you bring that effort every single day, that's where transformation happens. That's how change occurs."
~ Jillian Michaels ~

When considering a new goal, many times we do not follow-through with it because the process seems so overwhelming. We look at the big picture with a wide-angle lens, feel intimidated, and over think which ultimately paralyzes our progress. To achieve success, regardless if it is in sport, career, academics, finances, or our personal lives, break the big picture down into smaller segments. A perfect example is this book you are reading. My goal was to write a book to help people redefine and rediscover their ultimate happy life, however inside of this book contains chapters, which breaks down this process. When writing, I have not become overwhelmed at all because I have focused on each chapter one at a time, which ultimately builds up to my goal of writing Happiness Rescue. If I tried to write the full book in one sitting, it wouldn't ever get done!

In "The 12 Week Year" by Brian P. Moran and Michael Lennington, they present a formula for goal setting that works. Instead of making a yearly goal every January 1, it suggests breaking the year into quarters, then into months, then into weeks. If you've ever made a New Year's Resolution, you understand how difficult it is to keep that resolution for a full year. For me, that just makes me feel like a failure every January 1st.

I am in the gym regularly, and I notice the number of bodies in the studios to be way more in January. But by Valentine's Day, the traffic drops off again. The yoga studio can get crowded, so I tend to avoid yoga the first 6 weeks of the year. I really don't enjoy my mat so close to the next person that I can hear the sweat dripping from their bums while in downward dog. But what happens after 6 weeks? People give up, and then make the same resolution the following year with no success.

I set goals, and I achieve them. In my coaching practice, my clients learn how to set and achieve their goals. We sit down together and work out a commitment plan, where we set goals, action items, rituals, check-in points, and celebration markers. My coaches did this for me as an athlete, and I have also worked with many top athletes to help them achieve their goals.

Goal setting is for everyone. Whether you're an athlete, stay at home mom, entrepreneur, small business owner, employee, or retired, we can all benefit from setting goals. Setting goals helps us focus, get out of our comfort zones and reach towards our dreams. The feeling of success builds confidence, positive morale, pride, and happiness, which enriches our lives.

"The 12 Week Year" duplicates the process that I used as an athlete, breaking down my goal into smaller chunks. Each season was broken into smaller sections, and I would decide what kind of training I would do each day and set check-in points to ensure that I was on track to meet my goal.

This process can be done for all goals. It's a system to follow and can be used with small or big goals. Say you want to lose ten pounds. This is a great goal, but remember that you also need to set a timeframe for accomplishing your goal. Your timeframe should be realistic and attainable, but also encourage you to stretch your limits. Losing ten pounds in 1 year is realistic, but it's not much of a stretch. If you're implementing your daily rituals, you should be able to safely lose ten pounds in 12 weeks. Now we write down our goal, print off a twelve-week calendar, and work backwards. We want to see the end result and work back to our start date. Put in any special events you have on your calendar, birthdays, Christmas, Easter etc. and also make sure to choose a "rest day" each week.

Now it's time to add checkpoints or micro-goals. At the end of the twelfth week, you would write the weight down you want to be when you reach your goal. Then figure out where you need to be on the eighth week: if you want to lose ten pounds in 12 weeks, you will want to lose at least 6 pounds by the end of week 8. By the end of the fourth week, you should lose at least 3 pounds. So, for each week, write down how much you want to weigh at the end of that week.

Now you have a basic structure. Add in the tasks you need to do to accomplish your goal. For losing weight, you'll need to exercise each day, excluding your rest day. Your exercise should include some weights and some cardio, maybe walking, riding your bike, swimming, whatever you prefer, but make sure you alternate your cardio days with your weight days. There you have it, which is pretty much your starting point and your exercise plan. You'll also need to cut back your calories 6 days a week — you have a cheat day so that you don't feel completely deprived and miserable.

All goals must be measured. I know you don't want to get on that damn scale and see how much you weigh, but to lose weight we must know our starting point and weigh yourself each week, on the same day and time so we are measuring it. Then we can determine if we are moving closer to or farther from our goal. If you're not moving closer, you'll need to adjust your plan: add in some high-intensity cardio or cut out additional calories.

Now you can visualize your twelve-week plan. You have broken your plan down to 3 individual months, with micro-goals and you have written each day, check-in assessment dates, your exercise routine, and your eating plan. The daily action items are your daily rituals, which will get you day by day to weighing ten pounds less in 12 weeks.

To make the most of your goal-mapping:

1. Believe
   Believe in yourself and knock that inner bully off your shoulder. If you truly desire something, do not let anyone hold you back, not even you.

2. Visualize your why
   Reaching your goal may be all exciting at the beginning but gets harder as time goes on. When it does get tough, rely heavily on your vision and visualize yourself already achieving your success. Always see yourself succeeding.

3. Do not delay
   If you have the desire to go for a certain goal, do not delay. Why wait? Don't live with regrets and don't live with excuses. If you do not know how to start or reach your goal, find some help, coaching and accountability to make it happen.

4. Write it down
   Research shows that people who write down their goals are 42% more likely to achieve them. Write your goals down and keep them where you can see them!

5. Plan of action
   You must have a plan. Having a goal without a plan is like driving to an unfamiliar destination without a map. Once again, keep your plan of action where you can see it, and when you're tempted to stray from it, remember why you set this goal in the first place and how great it will feel to accomplish it.

6. Commit to your daily rituals
   Commit to your rituals every day, including your action steps. If you miss one, don't beat yourself up, but re-commit to your goal the next day. Do not allow yourself to take the rest of the week off just because you missed one day. Imperfect action is better than no action at all.

7. Stay focused
   Use your plan of action to stay focused. When I was training full time, I could visually see where I was in the process and how I was doing. This helped me stay motivated. Use affirmations, visualization, positive cue-words, or any other tool, which will help you focus and stay on target.

8. Check-in points
   You have micro-goals, which you strive for, but check-in points take all the markers and variables through an assessment, so you can figure out what is working and what is not working. Maybe you absolutely hate the bike and it is making your exercise program painful for you, so adjust it at the check-in point. Try the elliptical for the next few weeks or the treadmill, whichever it is, as long as it is accomplishing the same task it will work in your plan.

9. Measure
   Measuring your progress is necessary. You won't know if your plan is working if you aren't measuring regularly.

10. Succeed & Celebrate
    Celebrate your successes, including the small ones! Celebrating feels good and will keep you motivated to stay on track. When my husband and I paid off our car loan, we celebrated by going out to see a local theatre group.

If you need any help with anything I have discussed in this book, please do not hesitate to reach out to me on my website at amandamaystark.com. I'd love to have a discussion and help you with your goals and ambitions.

CHAPTER SIXTEEN

TO DO LISTS FAIL, SUCCESS LISTS SOAR

"Long hours spent checking off a to-do list and ending the day with a full trash can and a clean desk are not virtuous and have nothing to do with success. Instead of a to-do list, you need a success list — a list that is purposefully created around extraordinary results. To-do lists tend to be long; success lists are short. One pulls you in all directions; the other aims you in a specific direction. One is a disorganized directory and the other is an organized directive. If a list isn't built around success, then that's not where it takes you. If your to-do list contains everything, then it's probably taking you everywhere but where you really want to go."

~ Gary Keller ~

We can break down many of our goals, habits and rituals even further into daily tasks. Our to-do lists can be an effective tool for getting things done or a list of things, which compound on top of one another and create more anxiety and stress in our life. How do you treat your to-do list?

There are many ways to utilize a to-do list. You can prioritize the top 6 things from most too least important and complete them one at a time. This worked for me for a while. I used a white board to add, erase, and progress, but over a short period of time managing my list became another task I had to do during my day, instead of a useful tool.

When we have way too many items on our to-do list we get overwhelmed and lose focus, which often paralyzes us in the process. After time, we also lose sight of our own personal growth, health and happiness as we are always in a state of being busy. A state of busy-ness is the first error that leads to a downward spiral. We end up lacking focus, getting easily distracted, having difficulty managing our time and trying to do too much when multi-tasking. All in all, being busy is not a great thing to be if you genuinely want to be productive and reach your goals.

When I first started my business there was so much to do that at the end of the day, I really hadn't accomplished anything other than add more things to the list. After 6 months of doing this and getting no further along I began to explore other alternatives to productiveness. What I discovered was I really wasn't focused on what I really wanted and instead of creating a hierarchy of importance, I gave everything as much value as the next thing. I became lost in the process and chased the next best thing or shiny object producing zero results and no income.

As an athlete, if I were to be doing everything and anything each day in my training I would have experienced burnout and injury so fast. For me to reach my goals and to see the results I was striving for I would plan my day and my to-do list was my success list.

After reflecting and learning from my mistakes, I reinvented my success list and threw away my to-do list. What is a success list, and how is it different from a to-do list? A success list is very specific. Instead of putting everything under the sun on it and getting overloaded with tasks that don't get you anywhere, you have a detailed, calculated priority list of tasks, which you complete purposefully and mindfully.

With a success list you avoid distractions and you become more focused. The success list is an essential tool to achieving your long-term goals. A success list also helps you avoid multi-tasking, which is the number 1 error people make when striving for their goals or personal happiness. They think the more they can get done in a day, is a good thing because it helps them feel accomplished. Have you ever talked to someone, your friend, relative or colleague and you ask them: "Hey, how are you?" They respond by "I'm great, I was so busy today. I took the kids to school, went to work, got all my stuff done at work, went grocery shopping, picked up the kids, fed them, took them to soccer, came home and finally I got to bed around 11:00 pm." They feel accomplished — but are they successful?

Most people are on the treadmill of life, controlled by their to-do lists and feel that being busy is healthy and productive. They are the most stressed, unhealthy, unhappy people I know. They are always out to prove something, to be super mom or dad, but at the end of the day they have not looked after themselves and ultimately have not done one thing to help them reach their own personal goals.

Multi-tasking is not a useful tool, and must be eliminated to achieve your goals. Multi-tasking splits priorities, focus, quality, and results in half. It really does not help you with your time-management — in the long run it costs you time. For instance, you are in a time crunch for cooking dinner, so you've got pots on the stove, you're making a salad, the doorbell rings and meanwhile you are talking to your mother on the phone. I'm stressed just reading that sentence! Slow down! Focus on cooking dinner. Let the person at the door go away and tell your mom you will call her back later. Then, turn on some relaxing music, grab a glass of wine, feel more peaceful, and enjoy yourself.

So, what do you do instead of multi-tasking? Follow the 80/20 principle. In a nutshell, you should focus on 20% of the activities, which provide you with 80% of your results. The 20% of the mindful tasks are going to be on your success list. You can eliminate the other 80%, which are the mindless tasks that don't move you towards your goal.

The key word here is *focus*. When you are working on a task, focus on that task until it is complete. Sit down and identify the few tasks, which will help you lose weight, grow your business, attract your perfect partner or create your happiness rescue. Then invest your time in these activities. The 20% is where you will achieve your goals, find success, be less stressed and live a happier life.

By starting your own success list, it will help you feel less stress, less rushed, calm your thoughts and once you become more comfortable with the process you will be able to spend less time on your "busy" tasks and more time on what is truly valuable and important.

Here are 3 valuable tips to consider when starting your own success list:

1. <u>One thing at a time and with full intention</u>
   There is no reason to put pressure on yourself by overloading your list. What is the first thing, the 1 thing you feel you need to get done, which will impact all the others, like a domino effect? If you strategically line up your list and hit on the first item, most likely you will knock off several other items.

   Focus on this 1 thing with intention. Feel the impact of the process and enjoy what is happening in the moment. If you can simply appreciate the moments, and feel gratitude for them then this is what happiness is all about.

2. <u>Leave your past behind as you plan your list</u>
Let old problems and to do items remain where they belong – in the past. No matter how many times you revisit the past, there's nothing new to see and it does not serve you or your future. Don't let what once happened get in the way of what is happening. Just because you've made mistakes does not mean your mistakes get to define you. If something important did not work yesterday, figure out what changes can be made today.

Tame your inner bully let it go and move on productively. You must make a conscious effort to do this, be positive with your self-talk; however, this won't happen automatically. You will have to be strong and say to yourself, "I don't care how hard this is. I don't care how disappointed I am. I'm not going to let my past problems get the best of me. I am going to take the lessons I have learned and move on with my life."

This is when and only when you will be able to see the sun from behind the clouds and discover happiness.

3. <u>Leave room to breathe and exhale</u>
One of the major reasons why people are not happy in their lives is because their success list only contains items of priority and action. Like when I was an athlete and now as a writer, I have learned to take a day off to rest and recover. To allow myself time to get away and discover new unplanned, creative, fun things, which

allows me to re-energize and ironically become more productive.

We cannot be productive, successful or happy if our schedules are so crammed with "what's next," as we never get a chance to stop and smell the flowers.

Make sure your success list contains blocks of time just for you. Organize yourself, but do not be so organized that you lose track of what's really important. You want to feel successful and happy, not overwhelmed and stressed.

It is very important to focus on your priorities, but take it and live it one moment at a time. We want to avoid excuses, so set yourself up for success not for failure. If you need to ask for help, and if you are feeling uncomfortable, stressed, or stuck in the process, back away. Relax, laugh, go for a walk and remember happiness was never discovered by being busy. Happiness is discovered from within you, so count your blessings, be grateful and do not forget to smile.

CHAPTER SEVENTEEN

LOVE YOURSELF MINDFULLY

"What we are today comes from our thoughts of yesterday, and our present thoughts build our life of tomorrow. Our life is the creation of our mind."
~ Buddha ~

"Love yourself first and everything else falls in line. You really have to love yourself to get anything done in this world."
~ Lucile Ball ~

"I think the saddest people always try their hardest to make people happy because they know what it's like to feel absolutely worthless and they don't want anyone else to feel like that."
~ Robin Williams ~

Lucile Ball and Robin Williams were incredible comedians. They made people laugh, and often laughed at themselves. Lucile Ball understood the importance of loving herself and was easily able to relate to her fans and audience. Robin Williams was always laughing on the outside, making sure everyone else was entertained, but that was just a veneer he showed people. No one, however, saw the inner pain he was in.

Mental health issues have impacted me, my family and over a billion people worldwide, so I cannot write this book without mentioning them and their impact on our overall feelings of fulfilment and happiness. If you choose to implement only one thing from this book, this is the one that will have the biggest impact on your Happiness Rescue.

Being healthy isn't just about physical health. I have always been an advocate of physical fitness, but as I get older, I am rapidly becoming aware of how important mental and spiritual well-being is to our overall health. The skills mentioned in this chapter and the following 2 chapters have helped me in my daily struggle with recovering from depression. If you are affected by mental illness, now or in the future, these are vital coping skills that will help you or someone you know deal with depression, anxiety, or any other mental illness.

Meditation is an important part of my daily life. At first, afraid of what others would think, I was a "closet meditator." I felt like sitting and doing nothing was not a productive activity. But now, after practicing for some time and taking some meditation courses, I can see the benefits of meditation. Meditation has a calming effect. It slows down my type-A personality and mind to a controllable pace.

There are many different forms of meditation, so what am I talking about? Truthfully, there isn't one "right" way to do it. What I can do is tell you what works for me. With a type-A personality and a mind, which doesn't slow down, meditation did not come easy to me. What helped was learning I did not have to stop thinking all together, but instead, observe my thoughts. You're giving your mind a job to do while practicing. To do this, I focus on my breath, breathing in through my nose and out through my nose. Keeping my thoughts focused on my breath helps my mind slow down and be attentive to the one task and not scattered all over. I sit in a comfortable chair with my feet on the ground, hands rested on my thighs and in a quiet location.

Meditation may be used with the aim of reducing stress, anxiety, depression, and pain, while increasing peace, perception and wellbeing. It is also one key way for you to begin loving yourself and feeling greater joy and happiness.

Your life is indeed the creation of your mind. Whatever you have in your life now is courtesy of how your mind works. If you are sad, frustrated, and depressed, this is because of your thoughts. The good news is that meditation works at a subconscious level to enable you to recognize that your thoughts are not the truth, and you don't have to believe them.

The suggestions you give to your brain, whether consciously or unconsciously, shape how you think and what you think becomes your reality. Think of any difficult time in your life, anything which triggered your stress and anxiety and how it may have thrown you into a turbulent time of depression and you shut yourself off from your life. This may have been a job loss, break-up, or financial issues. During the crisis you may have removed yourself from your day-to-day life, using escapism and avoidance to get through the tough times. When I got laid off, I told everyone I was okay. I even said that it was the best thing that happened to me! But deep down, I was emotionally devastated by the impact and change it had on my life. This was when I started to meditate, as it was a way for me to begin to be kind to myself.

We often treat ourselves like our own worst enemy. After I got laid off, my inner bully was at her worst. I would never treat someone else with such harsh criticism or abuse! When you reflect on a time of crisis, how did you treat yourself? Were you kind and gentle or mean and critical of yourself? Did you try to change your negative thoughts to positive reinforcement or did you regularly talk down and judge yourself? If you were to treat yourself like your best friend and be kind, you probably would have quickly got over whatever the difficult issues that were plaguing you.

The thoughts you think directly affect your reaction and your state-of-mind to recover from life's ups and downs. If you can change your thoughts to a positive frequency to become less threatening and more supportive, you will be happier, and start to love yourself.

Meditation is a practice, which improves your state of awareness and empowers you. It is also a tool, which helps you slow down your mind and your thoughts. Over time, meditation will help you understand your mind, so you will recognize it when it is being a bully and know not to believe it. The thoughts are still there, but you won't react to them or act as if they are true. Instead you will just laugh and say, "Oh, there's the bully again!" This takes away any power that those thoughts have over you. It's not just our thoughts, but also our reaction to our thoughts, that shape our reality.

As mentioned above, meditation is a practice. Be kind and not hard on yourself. When you start to learn meditation, start with 5 minutes and gradually, each week or 2, increase the duration of your practice. This also reduces the pressure on yourself to put aside a huge block of time for a skill you are just learning, and in the long run you will be more likely to continue to meditate. There is absolutely no one-way of practicing meditation. If you are new to it, there are a few suggestions to begin and you may adapt or adjust it pending your preference as you become more skilled and confident.

If you have never meditated before there are certain things you need to know and from that point, you can modify them to suit your own personal practice. When you sit down to meditate, you may sit on a cushion, on the floor, or in a chair. Your back should be straight. You can rest your hands on your thighs. I prefer to sit with my palms facing up, middle finger and thumb softly touching. Relax your shoulders and open your chest. Adjust the angle of your head so the back of your neck is relaxed, with your chin slightly tucked in. Close your eyes or keep them slightly open and focus on one spot in front of you.

When you meditate, you will experience "monkey mind." Your mind is like a monkey, jumping from thought to thought just as a monkey jumps from one tree branch to another. You'll be amazed at how difficult it is to concentrate! Understand that this is completely normal, and you are not crazy. If you can't stay focused for very long, that's okay! The more you meditate, the more you will learn to calm the monkey mind.

While you are meditating, you will have thoughts. You will get distracted. That's your monkey mind. When you notice that you are not paying attention, turn your attention back to the focus of the meditation (your breath, a word, a visual cue, or a sound). Be kind to yourself when you catch your mind wandering. Over time, you will learn to calm your monkey mind, so you have more control over your thoughts, feelings, and emotions.

Do not try to control the monkey mind, but rather accept it and give it a task to focus on. If you can give it one thing to concentrate on at a time and teach it not to bounce around from thought to thought, you are one step closer to complete mindfulness. This will enable you to have a stronger focus of attention, be more productive for daily rituals, and help you achieve your goals. Maybe one of your goals is to slow down in your life, and this is the perfect skill to teach you how!

The most important component to meditation is to practice it like any other practice. Be consistent and be kind to yourself! When people start meditating, the inner bully often comes out, so this is a helpful reminder to be gracious and patient. We will not all be perfect the first time and it will probably feel uncomfortable and awkward at first. Remember, it is about progress, not perfection. To grow, we must begin to step outside our comfort zone. Take these signs as part of your growth as we do not improve or get better at anything being comfortable. Meditation is a critical tool to visualizing life's success, loving yourself, and becoming happy, so have fun and enjoy the process.

There are many tools to help with your meditation. One tool I love is Insight Timer, which is a free app. There is so much you can do with it — you can find other meditators near you and you can add friends. At the time of writing this book, the app contained over 11,000 free-guided meditations of all lengths, which you can bookmark or search based on your mood or energy. If you prefer to mediate in silence, you can use it as a timer, and it keeps track of how often and how much you meditate. You can go directly to iTunes,

Google Play on Android or you may go to insighttimer.com and source it from there.

I have also developed a few personal meditations, and I have one called *Happiness is Within You*, which is 10 minutes in length. You may download it here for free and I hope you enjoy it.
bit.ly/HappinessWithinYou10min

Additionally, here is a great YouTube video where a Buddhist monk explains with humour, insight and graphics "How to Train Your Monkey Mind."
youtu.be/n6pMbRiSBPs

CHAPTER EIGHTEEN

MAKE IT HAPPEN WITH VISUALIZATION

"Visualization is the process of creating pictures in your mind of yourself enjoying what you want. When you visualize, you generate powerful thoughts and feelings of having it now. The law of attraction then returns that reality to you, just as you saw it in your mind."
~ Rhonda Byrne ~

"Proper visualization by the exercise of concentration and willpower enables us to materialize thoughts, not only as dreams or visions in the mental realm, but also as experiences in the material realm."
~ Paramahansa Yogananda ~

Visualization has played an enormous role in my life. Visualization has helped me overcome obstacles, achieve my goals, recover from tough times, and triumph throughout my life. As an athlete, mom, wife, and entrepreneur, visualization was the key tool I used to reach any and all goals in my life. In alignment with meditation, visualization brings focus, calmness, and offers a road map of how to get there. Visualization is an inner GPS for you to set your course, see your destination and navigate the direction of how you will get there.

Meditation and visualization may sound like the same thing, but they are not. Meditation is paying attention to what is, to the way the world is in this moment. Visualization is actively picturing a defined situation. Meditation is about giving the body deep rest to heal stress and calm the mind. Visualization, on the other hand, gives the mind a specific direction for a desired result, such as what we want in our lives, what we want to overcome (for example an illness), or what we want to avoid in our lives.

When we meditate we are aiming to get to a state of stillness, whereas visualization requires the brain to be active. You are more in control of the experience during visualization than if you are meditating. When visualizing, you use your imagination to have a full sensory experience of how your situation will play out.

Michael Phelps, the most successful and most decorated Olympian of all time, used visualization throughout his career. In fact, I do not know a successful athlete who does not use visualization. In 2016, Michael Phelps said he had been taught at a very young age to visualize. For him, he imagined how he wanted the race to go, how he didn't want it to go, and how it could go. In 2008 when he was going for yet another gold medal during his 200-meter final, his goggles filled up with water for 175 meters of that race. Instead of panicking and losing, he remembered what he had visualized, which was how he didn't want it to go. Pictured already in his mind was the scenario of his goggles filling up, so in his mind he had already been in the situation. This meant for him he was prepared and did not panic. Remarkably, he ended up winning the race, won gold, and broke the world record!

The power of visualization is life changing. As the popular saying goes, a picture is worth a thousand words. If we can see it, we believe it and that is the way visualization works. Everything we have talked about in Happiness Rescue is how you can discover, reclaim and recreate your inner happiness. Yes, you must ditch the past, eliminate self-doubt, be grateful, wipe out limiting beliefs, and set goals. But all of these can happen faster and easier with visualization. Imagine how you will feel when you don't have any self-doubt. What will your life look like? Visualization is the first step to realization.

Although I never got to the level of success Michael Phelps did, the success I reached in my sport was a tribute to my visualization practices. I scheduled visualization into my daily training schedule just as I did court, track and gym work. In fact, with all the insecurities I had, I can attribute my consistent, quality visualization skills as one of the main reasons for my success. I saw myself winning. I saw myself playing the national finals with a fractured ankle. I saw myself hitting the ball to the target successfully every time. I saw the venue I was going to play at, the court I would play on, the crowd who would be there, and even what I would be wearing at particular events. I was just as prepared as Michael Phelps.

Visualization can be used as a personal and professional development skill-set in everyone's life. If you are preparing for a business event such as public speaking, business negotiations, or a job interview you can use visualization to prepare yourself, so you know what to expect and how you would like the outcome to be before you walk in the room. Personally, visualization can be used in any situation. If you want to lose 10 pounds, run a 5-mile race, buy a new house, improve a relationship, overcome depression, or walk into a room full of strangers at a women's networking event, visualization is the key to helping you achieve anything you desire.

In my experience, there are 2 ways to practice visualization. The first is inner body and the second is outer body. What I mean by inner body is you feel yourself doing the action as if you were physically performing the task, in your own body. The outer body technique is when you are visualizing yourself performing the skill as if you are watching yourself from up above, outside your body. Either technique works just as well as the other; however, it is a personal preference and some people respond to one more than the other. With both techniques, you will experience the sensation of actually going through the motion, feeling the emotion and seeing the outcome of whatever it is you are imagining. Personally, I respond better to visualizing as inner body. I like to feel myself inside my body doing the action instead of seeing myself from above.

You can visualize anywhere, anytime, and anyway you are comfortable. For me, I am in the moment of doing the activity when I am seeing myself accomplish something. In my role as a Mindset and Well-Being Coach, I often get the opportunity to speak in front of audiences. Speaking in front of strangers does not come naturally to me, however, as long as I am prepared, the outcome is successful. The event does not start with an informative, entertaining, and interactive presentation. The event begins weeks ahead of time in my mind. I am imagining and seeing myself standing up on stage in front of dozens of women presenting to them and showing them how to become happier and live their best life. In my mind, I go through the presentation slide by slide while I drive my car, while I'm watching television, while I am walking my dogs, and I am mentally rehearsing my performance. The more I visualize, the more confident I become, and my insecurities become less. When I get to the event, I know I will be prepared because in my mind I have already been there.

The skill of visualization, similar to meditation, gets easier as you practice it more and more. It can be a fun part of your day as you play with your imagination and visualize what it is you desire most in the world. For example, if one of your goals is to lose 10 pounds you can implement the practice of visualization to help you get to your goal.

Alongside eating clean, exercising consistently, and drinking more water, begin to visualize yourself 10 pounds less. Imagine what you will wear, how you will feel and put yourself inside that lighter body you are so proud of. Make sure you visualize yourself in the present not in the future; as if you have already dropped the weight and can fit into those new blue jeans you just bought, which are 2 sizes smaller. Visualize how your partner will react to your new, lighter physical form, and how you now radiate an increased confidence and sexuality, something your partner has not seen in years. How exciting it is!

My youngest son is now going through university and is faced with so many challenges. Exams, assignments, grade expectations, finances, time-management, relationships, and the pressure to do it all as best he can are only part of the difficulties he faces. We have talked about visualization and he is now using it to help himself manage all of the tasks and expectations he tries to balance. He sees himself writing the exams, prepares his time-management, and foresees interruptions and obstacles. By foreseeing obstacles he can prepare solutions ahead of time. When they do happen he knows exactly how to handle them. In the bigger picture, in his mind, he walks the graduating stage, receives his degree, and plans his future. It helps him stay focused, avoid distractions, be proactive each day, so he can reach his dream of being a teacher!

Visualization is an incredibly powerful skill, which I encourage everyone to use in their life. It can be a powerful tool that helps you get everything done on your success list or achieve your biggest goal. In everyone's Happiness Rescue, visualization is the pinnacle skill, which will get you living your best life. See it, rehearse it, do it!

Below are 3 visualization techniques you can use to increase the quality of your mental imagery:

1. Picture and describe what your image
   The more details you have in your visualization the more real it will seem and you are more likely to believe it. For example, if you think about a piece of cake, but immediately dismiss the thought, you will quickly forget about it. However, if you think about the piece of cake, by closing your eyes and spend a few minutes really imagining the details, the creamy frosting, the moist cake, how wonderful it would taste, savoring the image until your mouth starts to water, your desire to get a piece of cake would dramatically increase.

   The best way to create detail of your imagery is to picture and describe it with all your senses. Keep adding more detail until the process starts to feel as real as if you were actually experiencing it.

2. Emotional intensity and feeling your vision
   The truer you believe something to be, the more emotional impact it has on you. To really enhance an image you want to create as much detail around it as you can, so that you begin to feel the experience of it, as if it were real. Once you begin to feel it, you have

crossed the threshold that leads to action. One strategy that increases the emotional intensity of visualization is to listen to music that matches the emotional intensity you are seeking as you are visualizing your simulated experience. If you want to run a marathon, try listening to inspirational music like the theme song from Chariots of Fire as you run across the finish line with everyone cheering!

3. <u>Exposure through experiencing your vision</u>
   Since what you produce in your mind can only come from what you have experienced or seen, it can be difficult to imagine something that has not already happened to you. It would be much more difficult to create a visual image of living on Mars, than it would be to visualize yourself standing in your living room.

Sometimes in order to create a detailed and realistic visualization in your mind, you have to expose yourself to more detail in the outside world. For example, if you really dream of doing something you've never tried before like scuba diving, you may have a difficult time simulating a detailed experience, since you don't have much to draw on. You will need to expose yourself to the experience of scuba diving. You may need to read books, watch videos, visit a scuba diving school, or talk to other people who have scuba diving experience. This would help you have more information to draw upon when creating your own visualization.

CHAPTER NINETEEN

YOUR LIFESTYLE SHIFT

"The formula of happiness and success is just being actually yourself, in the most vivid possible way you can."
~ Meryl Streep ~

"Even when someone gets to looking like she should be so proud of herself; instead she's like, 'I could be another three pounds less. I could be a little taller and have bigger lips.' Where does it end? You just have to say, 'It's pretty damn good. I am right here at the moment and I'm okay with it."
~ Melissa McCarthy ~

"At the end of the day, you won't be happy until you love yourself."
~ Lady Gaga ~

Physical fitness is one of the most important rituals you can schedule into your day. Regardless of your age there are so many benefits to being physically active. Physical fitness is not just good for the body; it also can improve your mind, relationships, self-esteem, mental health and happiness.

Whenever I joined a new diet or fitness program, I had to take a before picture. I had to undress down to my underwear and bra and take pictures of myself from different angles. I felt shamed and humiliated, but I did it because I was told that it was the first step to change. In my quest for happiness, this certainly didn't help. I wasn't becoming happier by putting myself through this painful exercise every time I started a diet. Instead, I just saw how out of shape and overweight I really was. I have a library of before pictures, but I have never taken any after photos, because I always quit the diet before I achieved my goal weight.

How does viewing ourselves half naked in front of the mirror bring us closer to happiness? All we are doing is judging and seeing ourselves for the external veneer of our physical form. Like going to the gym and comparing ourselves to the next person beside us, we are now comparing ourselves to how we perceive ourselves to look. If we do not have a positive mindset about ourselves, no matter how we look in the mirror will never be good enough. What we think creates our thoughts, creates our feelings, which leads to either a positive or negative view of ourselves.

The sad part is that this approach rarely succeeds, because we are only looking at the outside. For true change, we need to take inventory of how we are and how we may need to shift our ways of thinking. Before we can change and become happier and more confident with our outer bodies, we must first spend time on our inner self.

For someone who is overcoming any form of mental illness, depression, anxiety, or life trauma, the number one benefit of exercise is survival. How good do you feel when you just sit on the couch for an entire day, let alone an entire weekend? When you binge watch Netflix, episode after episode, eat junk food, and only get up to use the bathroom, how do you feel about yourself?

How much social interaction do you get from just watching TV? How much brain stimulation do you get from just going to work pounding out deadline after deadline, going to one meeting after another? At the end of the day, you feel like your brain got fried at work, and you're exhausted. Where have you taken time to breathe, exhale, get the blood flow going and taken time for yourself?

This book isn't about becoming an elite athlete who trains twelve times per week and has no other responsibilities other than to keep themselves in shape. Exercise benefits everyone, especially those who are stressed, tired, stuck, a little or a lot overweight, and who need motivation, inspiration and a purpose to smile. Exercise is one of the most important things you can do to start being *you*, the person you know who is hiding inside of you, the one who wants and deserves a Happiness Rescue.

Exercise is not just about weight loss. The many benefits of exercise include: boosting brainpower, releasing stress, increasing your metabolism and energy level, and warding off disease. And these are only the physical benefits! Exercise can also improve your relationships with others. Exercising with a group of people can give you a new social outlet and new friends. Oh, and exercise increases your libido too!

Exercise can also build strong family relationships. When my sons were young, if I asked them how their day was as we sat around the dinner table, their answers would be short. "It was fine," or "Nothing happened." But when we were active as a family, they opened up. When we played badminton, or went for walks, they would freely talk about school and how their lives were. Exercising together made our family very strong, and that strong communication dynamic continues today.

Beginning a successful exercise program starts with developing your daily rituals to achieve your optimum health, wellness, and success. The hardest thing about any ritual, habit or routine is starting. Once you start, consistency is the key to success. Even if you don't see the results you wanted right away, it's important to stay consistent with your rituals.

One program I offer is called the 28 Day Fit-For-You Self-Challenge. In 28 days, the challenge helps people develop a consistent routine, which includes cardio, stretching, and meditation. Regardless of where you are starting, the challenge can help you become consistently active, more mindful, and in better shape in only 4 weeks. There's also a social component, a private online group where people gather for increased support, laughter and motivation. After 28 days, these participants are now exercising 6 days a week, and have a routine that they can maintain.

What makes this program different? Instead of focusing on how you look (like in the before and after pictures), we focus on the inner work first. There's daily meditation, and a consistent routine. Remember it is not about the after picture; this is about developing a skill, a ritual in your day, which is just for you. This is one way for you to put yourself higher up on your success list and begin to feel satisfied and proud of yourself.

When you are starting to exercise, keep these ten things in mind:

1. <u>Think of it as a lifestyle shift, not a program</u>
   Once you call something a program, it sounds so much more serious. This is a lifestyle shift. Similarly, instead of going on a diet, begin eating healthy, and make that part of your routine. You are being kind to yourself and focusing on making lasting changes. A program and a diet go for a certain period of time and have a beginning and an end date. A healthy lifestyle is just that, small healthier decisions or rituals you do every day to reach your goals.

2. Start small
   You don't have to go to the gym for one hour every day! If you only have 15 minutes, use that time to get quality exercise. Focus on cardio and be mindful of what you're doing and how you feel.

3. Be kind to yourself
   A gym can be intimidating. With all the mirrors, spandex, crop tops and ponytails, it is challenging not to compare yourself to everyone around you. Instead, the next time you look in the mirror, smile and give yourself a wink. Congratulate yourself for being there and ignore your inner bully.

4. Pick an exercise you enjoy
   Don't torture yourself. Try different kinds of exercises to see what you like. I can't stand treadmills, but occasionally I have to use one. So, I make it enjoyable by mixing it up. I walk backwards and sideways. It makes my mind think differently, get outside my comfort zone, and work other muscles. People stare at me, which makes me laugh, and I feel great!

5. Grab an exercise buddy
   Unless you are self-motivated and enjoy the isolated time with your headset on, exercise is more fun with a friend. Phone a friend, make them come with you and push each other. Reward yourself after by hitting the cafe for a smoothie or an iced coffee.

6. Get outside with a dog
   Maybe you're not a gym person. That's okay. In the summer, I do as much as I can outside, walking and

playing with my dogs. It makes them happy, to be outside and interacting with others. Don't have a dog? Borrow one from a neighbour or volunteer at the shelter. You will never get a dog who does not want to go for a walk or run and they are the best exercise buddies!

7. Allow yourself one day of rest
You need a rest day. You need to take one day off a week to recharge, be lazy and chill-out. It is good for your muscles to recover, but it's also good for your state of mind. Plan an enjoyable day off, get jobs done, allow yourself your Netflix day and then prepare to get going again the next day.

8. Listen to a book or a fun playlist
Exercising alone? You can make it more interesting by listening to an audiobook (with audible.com you can download books straight to your phone). If audiobooks aren't your thing, create a fun and motivational playlist of songs you love. Bopping to your favourite tunes during your workout session is incredibly satisfying and before you know it you are looking forward to the next one.

9. Focus on what you can do, not what others are doing
You might see someone power-walking like an Olympian, but that doesn't mean that you have to do the same! Be kind to yourself. Push yourself so you step outside of your comfort zone, but don't force yourself to do the same things that others are doing. You do not need to battle against anyone else. Just

because the slim cutie is pounding it out on the treadmill at 7 miles per hour, doesn't mean you have to. Do what is right for you. You are creating a healthy, happy life. You will definitely *not* be happy when you fly off the back of the treadmill trying to compete with the cutie. Focus on you and no one else.

10. <u>Get out of the gym. Try yoga, get outside, or go to the pool or squash court.</u>
You do not need to be in the gym to exercise 6 days a week. Mix it up. Try the gym twice, a long walk outside, yoga, squash, and swim once a week. There are your 6 days. Mixing up your routine does wonders for versatility and stimulation. Shuffling your exercise regime will help you get better results. You will not only avoid being bored, but you will be working on different muscles and body parts each day. This will give you increased physical benefits and results.

If you are interested in the 28 Day Fit-For-You Self Challenge, please reach out to me on my website at amandamaystark.com and we'll discuss if the program is right for you.

CHAPTER TWENTY

FINDING GRATITUDE

"This is a wonderful day. I've never seen it before."
~ Maya Angelou ~

"Gratitude is a powerful process for shifting your energy and bringing more of what you want into your life. Be grateful for what you already have and you will attract more good things."
~ Rhonda Byrne ~

In the quest for happiness, we need to spend a lot of time and emphasis on learning to love ourselves and our self-care. One of the best ways to undo old thinking patterns and train your brain to think in new ways is to start a gratitude journal.

A gratitude journal is a notebook where you give thanks and appreciation for the gifts you receive from the universe or from God, whichever you believe. It is your diary of the blessings in your life. Notice them as they happen and as you desire them to happen. When you are mindful and paying attention, the universe is listening.

For this book and as a spiritual reference, I speak of the universe as a higher power greater than we are as human beings on this planet. For clarity, the universe is by no means mentioned to dismiss any other belief or conviction. Some people call this force God, and others don't. However, I believe if we trust and have faith in this higher power of our creation we can put our wishes, desires and feelings out there where they will be received and answered.

When I was young, I used to write in a diary. My diary was one of those cute, pink, flowery diaries with the little lock and key on it. I wrote all my "secrets" in my diary including my school crushes and my moment-by-moment moods of my early adolescence. My diary was so precious and safe, even from my sister and my mom since they didn't have the key.

A gratitude journal is like a diary. You can even buy a cute, pink, flowery diary with a lock and key for your gratitude journal if you'd like! But a plain notebook will do just as well. What really matters is what you write in it. Your gratitude journal is about giving thanks and feeling grateful for what is currently in your life and your vision of the future. It is a tool you use to show gratitude for what you currently have and to record your vision of what you desire in your future.

Your gratitude journal is where you record all the blessings in your life, including those that you may think of as small and unworthy. Maybe your child said something funny, or your dog did something cute. Or it could be something as simple as not having to wait in line at the grocery store! It is incredible if you sit quietly once a day and reflect on everything you did that day. When you feel gratitude, you are on your way to a happier life.

So, what if you had a terrible day? Then what do you write in your gratitude journal? Even if your day was terrible, you can probably find something to be grateful for. You could take your biggest challenge and be grateful you overcame it. For example, building my business has really had its challenges. There are days when nothing works the way it's supposed to, including my website or online course platform. On those days, I am grateful for the people who can solve technology issues, since that is not my forte.

Here's another example: one day I ran into a roadblock recording a new personal meditation and it was incredibly frustrating. I was having challenges understanding how to edit the content and how to mix the music with my voice. With any new software or application, it takes time to understand. I searched the problem on Google and YouTube and found some incredible resources, which clarified exactly how to do it. In the end I persevered, figured it out and at the end of the day I noted how grateful I was to have been determined enough to finish it.

You are also going to write the things you are grateful for in your vision of the future. Now I am not a grandmother (yet), however, with my son recently being married I have plans for when I am blessed with a grandchild. I want to help my son and his wife with childcare and to be a huge part of my grandchild's life. Unfortunately, I personally did not have a consistent relationship with my grandparents as they lived in Australia and we were in Canada. Therefore, it is my vision and is very important to me to be able to be a loving, fun grandma to my children's children.

Another example of your future vision may be "I am so grateful I no longer speak negatively to myself and I accept myself for the person I am." This is an entry for myself, and quite possibly for you as well (in other words, I'm grateful that I no longer listen to my inner bully). So, I write it in my gratitude journal, putting it out to the universe; to become grateful for who I am and accept this to be true.

The structure of your gratitude journal is very personal. But whatever you do, make sure you include the wonderful things that you are grateful for now, as well as what you see for your future. Also, be consistent with your journaling. Maybe you like to write down the things you are grateful for in the morning, when you first wake up. Or maybe you prefer to write them in the evening.

Regardless of when you do them, be consistent. Make your gratitude journal a part of your daily ritual.

Here are 5 tips and suggestions for you to start, utilize, express and record a gratitude journal for your own happiness rescue. Keep in mind that nothing you write in your journal is silly, or embarrassing. Your journal is your safe place to be who you are. It is an incredible tool for you to begin and continue to build on your confidence, self-expression, self-love and overall life happiness.

1. You do not have to buy a fancy diary or expensive journal. You can if you want, or you could go to your local dollar store and pick up a notebook. Voila! You have yourself a gratitude journal.

2. Do not put a date in your gratitude journal, as the universe knows no time. When you record time, you are giving it a limitation. When writing in your gratitude journal you want to eliminate the limitations because as we know, we are putting everything out there to believe, achieve and feel grateful for in the moment without limiting our emotion.

3. Start with the left side page. On this side of our journal is where you write about 4-6 things, experiences, emotions, people, pets, nature etc., which you were grateful for that day. You may say something like, "I am grateful for the beautiful day today as the sun was shining and I went for a long walk feeling the sun on my face."

Start each submission with "I am grateful for_____" or "I am so thankful for_____" or "I have so much gratitude for_____." You see, each of these are in present tense and express your gratitude or thanks for something, which touched you or made an impact on you. Once you have written 4-6 entries, quietly say to yourself "thank you, thank you, thank you" as a gesture to the universe or to yourself.

4. Moving to the right side of your journal, directly across from your daily thanks and appreciations, is your future and what you see for your future. On this side, you will look ahead, with your own vision and write 4-6 entries of things, people, experiences, and desires for your future. Use the same structure: "I am grateful for _____" or "I am so thankful for _____" or "I have so much gratitude for _____." For example, one of my visions is "I am so grateful I am now a grandmother and I have such an incredible relationship with my grandchild as I babysit them every Friday." Once you have written 4-6 entries for your future, close your journal and end your session with repeating for a second time "thank you, thank you, thank you" to the universe or to yourself.

5. Be consistent! Make sure you are consistent in writing in your gratitude journal. Consistency in everything you do in life is imperative to making things happen. If you only workout once a week, chances of you getting into shape are much slimmer and slower than if you worked out 5 or 6 times a week. The same is true for writing in your gratitude journal. Make it an evening

ritual to spend 5 or 10 minutes each night reflecting, giving thanks and feeling grateful by writing in your journal.

A gratitude journal is only as effective as you believe it to be. You can write things down, however if you do not believe them to be true, the universe will pick up on this and will not believe it either. Your negative self-talk, or self-chatter as you put pen to paper will resonate onto the paper and stall the process. If you're in a bad mood, try a short meditation before you journal, or do something else to put yourself on a higher frequency. Going for a walk, having a bubble bath, or painting your nails may be options for you to get out of your mood. What works for me is a meditation and I created one for myself called *Beautiful Mind*, and I'd like to share it with you. You can listen to it or download it at bit.ly/BeautifulMind10min. Good vibrations and frequency with your desires is imperative for manifesting what you really want and your aspiration for a happy life. Receiving these things takes work and positive emotions.

Beautiful Mind Meditation:
bit.ly/BeautifulMind10min.

With each submission you exchange positive frequencies into the universe and the universe is listening. Writing them down and then letting them go, will be rewarded in some way, whether you are paying attention or not. In my opinion, we take so much for granted. Our health, friends, family, jobs, pets, homes, sight, hearing, breathing are all wonderful things. We go through our day and pay no tribute to the blessings we have.

If you can do one ritual each day to make yourself happier, it would be to slow down, give thanks, and feel grateful for what you have by writing in your gratitude journal. I encourage you to start today and if you have any questions please do not hesitate to reach out to me via my website at www.amandamaystark.com.

CHAPTER TWENTY-ONE

LEARN TO LAUGH AGAIN

"From there to here, from here to there, funny things are everywhere."
~ Dr. Seuss ~

"When we can begin to take our failures non-seriously, it means we are ceasing to be afraid of them. It is of immense importance to learn to laugh at ourselves."
~ Katherine Mansfield ~

One day after I got laid off from my job, I went for a walk. I saw a squirrel running along a fence and my dog took off after it (we were in an off-leash area). The squirrel started messing with my dog, teasing her and playing "catch-me-if-you-can." My dog was going crazy! I found myself laughing at the squirrel's antics and my dog's reactions. Laughing felt so liberating. Over the past few years, I had forgotten to laugh, and I realize now how important laughter is.

It sounds so sad, but I really had forgotten to laugh out loud. I'm talking about real belly laughter, the kind that's full of pure and innocent joy and happiness. The unconscious form of laughter, which is not forced, controlled or expected, but comes from the inner core of oneself. Laugher is the liberty simply to let go and enjoy oneself without judgement, thought, or apprehension.

With life's pressures, expectations and responsibilities weighing us down, we can get caught up in our jobs, worries and stress. We forget to laugh and experience joy. If you are fortunate enough to be around young children, just watch and learn from them. They can let it all go without thinking. The smallest thing can make them giggle or have fits of hysteric laughter. Watch them for a while and you too will feel so much lighter. I bet you'll even laugh! Their joy is so innocent that it can soften the hardest heart.

Joy and happiness are contagious, like grumpiness and sadness. What you or the people around you show on the outside will soon be felt by those around you. When you are around young children, or dogs, it's easy to get caught up in their joy. But if you spend your time with people who are worried, stressed, and unhappy, then you will feel it too.

Think about this. One day, you are at home and you're in a great mood! The day has been going your way, and you're happy. But then your family member comes home in a terrible mood. They had a bad day or got stuck in traffic on the way home. Then they feel grumpy, take it out on you. What suddenly happens to your mood? Yep, I'll bet you begin to feel grumpy and upset.

Living with someone who has untreated depression is the same. For the most part they are down in the dumps most of the time. Those they are close to, including the people who live with them, their friends, and their coworkers are in a constant state of pick-me-up. When someone is depressed, they struggle to see the positive in anything, and it is difficult to feel good around people like that.

Becoming aware of how you act and react to people, situations and experiences around you is very important in your quest for happiness. This is easier said than done, but it's necessary. When we take things too seriously, that not only affects our life, but also the lives of those around us.

Even during serious situations, you can take control of your reactions. My layoff affected my livelihood for a long time, and impacted my spouse. I did not get a very large severance package and I could not find another job, so I was really stressed. I could not control the outcome, but what I did have control of was my reaction to it. At the time, I was unaware of the control I did have, and I let my situation spin me into a downward spiral of depression. I gave my immediate situation far too much power. Very soon negative self-talk, my inner bully and pessimism crept in.

Working with a life coach and my doctor, I have become aware of my reactions. I learned skills that help me recognize when I am falling into "victimhood" mode. Victimhood mode is when you feel like you are a victim of circumstances, and you give up all power and control that you do have over the situation. Over time, I discovered how to get myself off the depression floor and back to myself and who I want to be; someone who is fun, content, smiling, carefree and truly happy.

Getting your laughter back is an unconscious reaction to how you are really feeling on the inside. If you are struggling to see the happy in life, here are 5 ways for you to get it back:

1. Daily nature walks
Schedule in daily nature walks. You'll become aware that the world is a bigger place than inside your own head. Breathe in the fresh air, look for animals, smell the flowers or the fresh cut lawn. If you live in the city, find a park and look for what nature surrounds you. The different kind of trees, birds and sounds you hear. Let nature help you relax, feel free and smile. Soon your smile will turn into a spontaneous laugh when you see the crazy squirrel playing games with a dog in the off-leash park.

2. Be mindful and live with intention
When we are mindful we are so much more aware of our surroundings and less focused on our own negative thoughts. When you are with your partner, children, colleagues, or by yourself, be present and in the moment. The past and future are only ideas; it is the present moment that is real. We live for the present

and we can decide how we react to it. Remember when you are mindful and live your life with intention, you become the maestro of your own experiences, your own happiness, and your own life.

3. Call a friend.
We all know at least one friend who, when we are around them, they just brighten our day. They happen to have an upbeat personality, who tends to be playful, can laugh and do not take themselves too seriously. Call them. Do not hesitate to call and be around people who are infectious with their smile, energy and optimism.

When you do call, make sure to keep the conversation light. This isn't the time for you to dwell on your negative feelings. Instead, ask how your friend is doing. Ask them what has made them laugh recently. Soon, you'll both be laughing, and you'll forget about the negative thoughts and emotions.

4. Remove the gloom
You are in control of the negative forces you engage with. Those forces may include people, news, or radio shows, or social media. You decide who you invest your time and energy interacting with. Find positive, encouraging influences to involve yourself with. If you are struggling, sometimes you find the best laughs when you are just by yourself.

5. Spend time with animals
If you are a lover of animals, there is no better way to feel better and laugh out loud than to interact with one.

This may be to take your own dog for a walk or play with your cat. If you don't have a pet, find another way to spend time with animals. Borrow one from a neighbour or volunteer at your local shelter. Or go on a nature walk and watch the wild animals! Animals are very focused on the present and can help us be mindful. They live a life full of innocence and joy. They can eliminate all our stress, anxiety, and sadness, even if it is only for a short time.

CHAPTER TWENTY-TWO

DROP THE CRUTCH

"Every addiction, no matter what it is, is the result of trying to escape from something by going in the direction of a need that is currently not being met. In order to move past our addiction, we have to figure out what we are trying to use our addiction to get away from and what need we are trying to use our addiction to meet."
~ Teal Swan ~

"It is by going down into the abyss that we recover the treasures of life. Where you stumble, there lies your treasure."
~ Joseph Campbell ~

One big challenge for me is my addictive personality. An addictive nature is one where it is difficult to find balance in routine, habits, time, family, work, or your favourite phone game. I focus on one thing and am unable to think about anything else. Some people would think this is a good thing, but addiction blinds me to anything else that is happening. I don't pay attention to what anyone else thinks, or even my own logical thoughts.

An addictive personality is not something that can be diagnosed, but it does alter your mind and make everyday life difficult. When I have experienced signs of addiction I am suspicious of my behaviour, but I do not listen or respond to my intuition. I have a strong sense of what is right and wrong, my addictive side of me does not. I ignore my gut, my family, and it is difficult to focus on what really matters.

Addicts do not know the difference between mild, moderate and obsessive use or participation in a substance or behaviour. Even young people can be addicts, as we see children tethered to their iPads and phones. Even healthy behaviours become unhealthy when someone is addicted. Exercising is good but exercising 16 hours a day isn't good for you. When behaviour becomes obsessive it negatively impacts other areas of your life, which end up suffering.

Throughout my Happiness Rescue, I was forced to look at my own daily habits. I realized that my evening alcohol ritual was interfering with my health and happiness. Throughout the week, I was drinking up to 24 drinks and waking up with a hangover at least 3 times per week. After speaking to my doctor, I realized quickly this was one area of my life, which had to change if I was going to ever be happy again.

Alcohol provided me with instant gratification and a false sense of euphoria. Alcohol made me feel good, relaxed, and numbed away any challenges I was dealing with. That sounds great, right? The problem was that alcohol had become a crutch in my life and I couldn't go through an entire day without it. I was leaning on it and could not cope with life without the aid of a few drinks.

My excuse for having 2 or 3 drinks every night was that this was how I had been raised. I was born in Australia, where beer was an essential component of the laid-back lifestyle. I was young when we moved to Canada. Growing up, my father would work until around 8:00 pm. When he came home, my parents would have 1 or 2 drinks to get caught up on their day. We waited to eat dinner until after he was home and had his drinks. Then I became an athlete, in a sport where alcohol was part of the social culture. Being a good athlete, I often spent time with older players who were drinking.

I carried these habits with me, into my adult life. Drinking alcohol is fine while you are in control and healthy. But one of the consequences of drinking is a lack of self-awareness, so many who drink consider themselves healthy even though they are not. When your health slips out of sync, you become unhappy, which leads to more drinking. However, once I realized how unhappy I was, I examined every pattern of my life and realized how much drinking was harming me.

After my "worst" day, I told my doctor about my drinking habits. She helped me understand the negative effects alcohol can have on depression. Together, as part of my recovery plan, we made drinking less a conscious, awareness choice. Honestly, it was one of the hardest parts of my Happiness Rescue because I had to face some addictive habits I was very comfortable with and which I felt made me feel happy. But when I realized how my drinking contributed to my depression, I knew I had to change.

After I stopped drinking every evening, my sons and I had a conversation about my depression. My oldest son said, "Mom, you are a much better mom when you are not drinking." *Wow*, talk about hitting home, straight and direct message there! I love my sons and I want to be the best mom I can be, so I still to this day take this statement very seriously.

I have not quit drinking entirely, but I have looked my drinking demon in the face and have come to terms with it. I have drastically limited my use of alcohol and now I actually enjoy the taste of a glass of wine and do not drink simply for the sake of drinking. If you think you may be addicted, ask yourself why are you drinking? Is it so you can feel better about your life? Or is it because you enjoy a glass of wine on occasion? Be honest with yourself!

If you have an addictive personality, becoming aware of it is key to your Happiness Rescue. Maybe you're addicted to alcohol like me, or maybe you smoke cigarettes or use drugs. Other activities like playing video games and even working can be unhealthy if you are addicted. Other addictive tendencies include gambling, sex, overspending, watching porn, overeating, and hoarding. This is not an exhaustive list — anything can be addictive if you focus on it to the exclusion of everything else.

Here are 5 ways for you to begin to drop the addictive crutch and take back full control over your decisions and stop hiding from your reality:

1. <u>Take responsibility for your actions</u>
   Own up to your instincts. If you feel you are doing something too much, or you are relying on a behaviour or substance too much, then take responsibility immediately. Confide in your partner, a friend, a life coach, a therapist or your doctor right away. Make a plan to change and commit to it. This way you will stop being a helpless victim and become a purposeful leader of your life. When you stop feeling helpless, and start taking charge of your life you won't need to turn to destructive behaviours anymore.

2. <u>Know your enemy</u>
   Know your vice, your crutch or your bad habit and the implications it might be having on your life. Attain such knowledge from your doctor, and do not rush so quickly to the internet as it contains so many unreliable sources. Take your enemy and your health seriously. If you have an addictive personality, it can be helpful to regularly ask yourself how well you are balancing the different responsibilities in your life and make any changes that are needed.

3. Be kind to yourself
   Once you have begun to own your own actions and take back control of your decisions, it is important to be your own cheerleader and best friend. If you have come up with a plan with your coach or doctor and you slip up or have a setback, do not beat yourself up. Remember, we are too hard on ourselves and our success in finding happiness will only happen if we are kind and forgiving, yet strong enough to get back on track right away.

4. Do not feel deprived
   Do not to tell yourself you cannot indulge in the things that you are trying to avoid. It will only make you feel more deprived, which in turn will make you think about what you are missing more. Instead, think about the negative impact these things had on your life in the past and say to yourself "I can have them, but I choose not to." You can also focus on the things you *can* have. Maybe you can't have a second drink anymore, but you can have a wonderful conversation with your spouse after dinner.

5. Shift your mindset
   Each time you break a bad habit, you are going to go through withdrawal symptoms. You may have physical and/or mental symptoms, and these are very challenging to deal with. By shifting your mindset, you are refocusing your thoughts to positive feelings. If you had an addictive tendency to eat food in the middle of the night, shift your thoughts. Before you go to bed hang a bathing suit on the fridge or cupboard. When

you do wake to go and eat, you'll second-guess your decision to indulge and it is those few extra seconds of thoughts that will begin to change your action to eat.

Shifting my mindset over alcohol was very difficult, but not impossible. When I think I would like a second or third drink, I remember what my son said to me. I have also seen my weight drop, which makes me incredibly happy. Knowing that my sons are proud of me and that I am losing weight is helping me feel the inner happiness I have been searching for. By shifting your mindset, you too can begin to feel an immediate sense of happiness.

CHAPTER TWENTY-THREE

REDISCOVER YOUR PASSION

*"There is no passion to be found playing small —
in settling for a life that is less than the one
you are capable of living."*
~ Nelson Mandela ~

*"If you feel like there's something out there that
you're supposed to be doing, if you have a passion
for it, then stop wishing and just do it."*
~ Wanda Sykes ~

Self-consciousness is the awareness of what others might think about us, especially anything negative. When we judge ourselves or judge others, we are inhibiting our own growth and our own journey towards happiness. We stop being spontaneous, we stop things we enjoy, and we invest more time on others than we do in ourselves. Without realizing it, time passes by quickly, and we are that much older, but not much wiser.

As I get older, I remember what I used to enjoy as a kid. From the age of sixteen, I focused so heavily on my sport, I stopped doing everything else. I also had an addictive personality back then, so once I started playing, I was all in. While this focus helped me achieve great things in my sport, I sometimes wonder how different my life would be if I had tried to maintain some kind of balance.

Since I no longer compete at the professional level, and my children are grown, I have the time to explore other activities I enjoy. I think back to what I liked to do as a kid. When I was in my early teens, I loved doing pencil-rendering pictures. So, I recently bought a sketchbook and some pencils, and I have started drawing again. I enjoy drawing because it's very meditative and creative.

In a quest to love yourself and find inner happiness, I challenge you to think back to your childhood, and remember the activities you enjoyed. To start, make a list of 10 childhood hobbies you once enjoyed. Who knows, maybe you were into woodworking, drawing, painting, sculpture, dancing, soccer, sewing, cars, writing, guitar or swimming. You can also think about things you have never tried but might enjoy doing now.

Exploring your youthful hobbies is a great way to rediscover your passions, to develop your self-esteem, meet new people, de-stress, focus and to do something just for you. When you are immersed in a hobby, you are focused on what you are doing, so the negative thoughts have no room in your head. A hobby is totally different than a job you have to do, because it is a personal passion and you are choosing to do it.

In other words, you're being positively selfish. In our regular life we often tell everyone yes and rarely say no, but we don't give ourselves the same courtesy. It is vital for self-love you put yourself first and make yourself part of your priority list. So, say YES to doing something you enjoy, even if it means saying NO to someone else.

You might feel a little uncomfortable at first. Some people think that hobbies are for children. But they are for everyone, and you are putting yourself first and spending time just on you and your self-care. It doesn't have to be just a time filler either, it can morph into a passion, which gets you excited, helps you recover from a long day, or gets your mind working. It helps you boost the quality of your life, which is so vital for your overall happiness.

But what if you're not particularly passionate about anything? Where do you start? First, realize that everyone has a passion and you just haven't discovered yours yet. Then think about all the activities you enjoyed when you were younger, and what you enjoy doing now. What brings you joy? How can you do more of that?

Here are 5 steps to discovering your passion and to begin having some well-deserved fun:

1. Start with a list of 10 hobbies you once enjoyed as a child

   Really brainstorm here. Include activities you liked when you were 10 and those you liked when you were 15. If you have trouble thinking of 10 hobbies, you can expand into your young adult years. What did you do when you were younger that you don't do now? And if you still can't think of 10 activities, think about things that you've always wanted to try but never have.

2. From your list of 10, pick your top 3

   These will probably jump out at you immediately. If you have difficulty choosing, think about which activities brought you the most happiness. At this point, it's important to focus on what you *want*. Don't let your fear get in the way. Maybe you loved doing gymnastics as a child but feel like you could never do that today and you're afraid of looking silly. Don't worry about it!

3. Choose one passion you can implement right away and you feel super excited about

   Of your 3 top activities, which is the easiest to implement? What can you start doing this week? If your top 3 activities are horseback riding, kayaking, and painting, and you live in the middle of a city with no horses or lakes, you'll probably choose painting. If your top 3 activities are knitting, writing, and tennis, these are all easy to implement, so choose the one that you are the *most* excited about.

4. Take action immediately
   Go out and purchase any supplies, find local classes and sign-up if required. Find out everything you can about your new venture. It is imperative you do this right away and not let yourself procrastinate or start doubting your decision.

5. Pen the time in your calendar
   Make your hobby a priority on your success list. It needs to become an incremental time block in your week, which you will not waiver on no matter what. This is your commitment to yourself and one, which you cannot and will not break.

   BONUS step. Have FUN! Relax
   Be okay with exploring and stop critiquing yourself. You can screw up; it is where you will learn to improve, to laugh, and to be happy.

I encourage you to complete the *Rediscover Your Passion Worksheet* at the back of this book. It offers you an opportunity to brainstorm and break your thoughts down to a specific passion for you to explore and pursue.

CHAPTER TWENTY-FOUR

BRANCHING OUT

*"Alone, we can do so little; together,
we can do so much."*
~ Helen Keller ~

*"You can tell who the strong women are. They are
the ones you see building one another up instead
of tearing each other down."*
~ Unknown ~

Who you associate yourself with is who you become. Community, network group, family, colleagues, whoever you invest your time with; these people will greatly influence your state of happiness and quality of your experience. I have struggled with surrounding myself with the right people my entire life. Growing up in a male dominated sport, I felt more comfortable around men than with women. It wasn't until I decided to change my life, proactively manage my depression, and discover my happiness that I began to understand the power of women.

I did have a few close female friends growing up, but they were also fellow squash players. Most of them represented our sport alongside me on the provincial or national team. At certain times throughout the year, my close friends became my competitors. For an hour or 2, when we were on the court, we were rivals. In between matches we would run around, goof off, and get into trouble, but when we walked on court against each other, it was all business. I needed the help and support that these friends gave me. My squash friends were there to spur me on and to push me. They were my toughest competition. Without pushing each other, we would never have reached the success we did. I am still in contact with these friends, and we have an incredible bond. In fact, one of my close squash friends is a very creative person, and she was the first person I turned to when I needed help designing the cover of this book. I am so grateful she agreed to support me, my book, and Happiness Rescue.

When we are feeling sad it is very easy to withdraw from our friends, family and support network. We may lose interest in calling our friends, meeting new people or exploring new interests. Branching out is really important and a vital component of your Happiness Rescue. It may not feel natural at the beginning and you may have to force yourself to do it, but after you do, I guarantee you will feel better.

Building your social network may seem like a large leap and you may struggle with anxious feelings or self-doubt. Your inner bully might tell you that you're not good enough or that people won't like you. Don't let your inner bully stop you! If you have the feeling it is time for you to branch out, then do it. This feeling is your intuition telling you that you are ready. Do not let your inner bully get in your way. Instead, take a deep breath and make it happen. Visualize yourself going out. What are you wearing? Where are you going? Who are you going to meet? Visualize walking into the room of strangers, or plan to bring a friend. What will you do when you get there? Socializing is an important part of your Happiness Rescue plan to build your confidence, eliminate your self-doubt, and expand yourself to the joys and power of women.

When you let your inner bully stop you, you are holding yourself back. Two years ago, I met an incredible life coach here in Calgary who has her own embracing women networking group. She is a keynote speaker at many events and is a best-selling author. I thought about reaching out to her to ask her questions about her business and to see if she had any suggestions for me to build my business. Sadly, I did not listen to my instincts and was held back by the fear of "what if?" What if she said no? What if she was not interested in helping me? What if she was so successful that she wouldn't want to talk to me? So, I didn't contact her.

A few weeks ago, I ran into a friend who is associated with the life coach. I mentioned that I really respected the coach and had thought about contacting her. She asked me why I had not called her. I explained my fears: that she wouldn't want to talk to me or that she was too successful to want to get to know me. Then I realized that I was letting my inner bully hold me back. Life will only pass you by unless you make it happen, and so I did. I picked up the phone and reached out to her. She was so incredible! We met for coffee where she gave me all sorts of tips and strategies and actually offered to include me in her network.

I quickly realized if I had contacted her when I first thought about it, she could have given me some great ideas, and I would have had 2 more years of friendship and networking. But because I chose to let fear stand in my way and procrastinated, she wasn't able to help me.

If you are not happy or feeling fulfilled and you do not force yourself outside your comfort zone, nothing will change. Living inside your comfort zone for too long may make you feel safe, but doesn't allow for growth. To grow and develop you must take that valuable step and face your fears. You must reach out and get involved in something, which you know will make you happy. You can discover (or re-discover) your hobbies or passions because there are so many networking groups available for us to tap into. Whether you live in the city or country, women love to gather. They love to drink coffee (or tea), they love to talk, they love to help, and they love to empower other women.

Websites such as Meetup.com are perfect ways for you to find meet up groups around any subject matter. You may want to learn to play the guitar, exercise more, scrapbook, build a business, apply make-up, whatever your interest there is a meetup group out there for you. When I began writing this book, I wanted to learn more about the book publishing business and network with other writers. I joined a meetup writing group that meets weekly at a local cafe. In most cases they are free to join, and they are an incredible opportunity for you to get out and begin to feel great about yourself.

Meetup groups are particularly important for those of you who work from home or are at home raising children. At times, you may feel secluded and it could be a whole week before you actually get out of your pajamas. Once you sign-up for a group, you have a commitment on your calendar and something that will get you out of your house and around people.

What if you can't find a group? Then you can start your own! As part of my Happiness Rescue plan, I have committed to start a group myself. This was a big move for me, but as I get more and more confident I am really enjoying every experience I have. In my coaching packages, I have the opportunity for group coaching. There are times when we can learn from each other. My clients and I meet online on our computers and we can all see and interact with each other. In many cases some people are in their pajamas having coffee, laughing, and feeling alive all together.

When women help women, in business and in their personal lives, we are so empowered. My husband is so happy that I am now getting out, doing things on my own, and meeting new amazing people. It gives our relationship another dimension we have never had. I now have many friends and meet new ones all the time. Life does not need to be a solo struggle, take a breath and jump, leap out of your comfort zone and connect with a few community groups so you can make new friends.

If you are unsure how to get started here are a few ways, which help me:

1. Decide why you want to meet others
   Do you want to discuss your hobby or passion? Or do you want to have coffee and get out of the house for a few hours? Maybe you want your children to have some playtime while you talk with other parents. Whatever the reason, there is a group nearby that you can benefit from.

2. Take action now
   Look online at Meetup.com, in your community newsletter, at your grocery store, your children's school, or your gym. If you open your eyes and become mindful when you are out, there are postings everywhere. Join the groups, put the meeting in your calendar, and go!

3. Face your fear
   Even though you have booked the meeting, you may still feel afraid to go. You can always back out, right? Don't! If you begin to have thoughts of regret or backing out, remember why it was you signed up for it in the beginning. Also, look ahead to how you will feel

about yourself if you don't go and how happy you will feel about yourself when you do go!

4. <u>Find others like you</u>
   You might walk into an event and feel insecure because you don't know anyone. Look around the room for the one or 2 people who you get a good vibe from, or maybe the other people who look uncertain. Walk over to them and say, "Hello." In most cases they too are feeling intimidated and will welcome you taking the lead and breaking the ice. Before you know it, you have met your first new friend.

5. <u>Open up and let yourself be heard</u>
   Challenge yourself at the event or group meeting to get involved. It can be as simple as asking a question, answering questions, or participating in the icebreaker at the beginning of the meeting. You do not have to be the one always vocalizing, but try taking another small step to become more confident and empowered. That is one more step toward your Happiness Rescue.

CHAPTER TWENTY-FIVE

LET YOUR INNER CHILD OUT TO PLAY

"It sounds corny, but I've promised my inner child that never again will I ever abandon myself for anything or anyone else again."
~ Wynonna Judd ~

"If you can dance and be free and not embarrassed, you can rule the world."
~ Amy Poehler ~

Mbuki-mvuki, a word in the Bantu language spoken in the Niger-Congo region of Africa means, "to shuck off one's clothes in order to dance" or "to shed one's clothing spontaneously and dance naked in joy." Whether you call it "dancing naked," "mbuki-mvuki," or anything else it doesn't matter — what's most important is that you do it!

Yes, you read it right. Dancing naked, also known as "mbuki-mvuki" in your living room (or your bedroom, or wherever you can find the space) will allow you to drop all your inhibitions and insecurities and permit you the opportunity to just let go.

Think about when you were about 3-8 years old. Remember jumping up and down on the bed while the music played? Or when your parents forced you to have a bath and you'd take your clothes off and run around naked? You didn't worry about who was watching or looking. All you were doing was having fun...and avoiding the bath.

Earlier, I talked about the innocent joy that children experience. That joy is available to everyone, not just children. But to feel it, you need to drop your adultness and release all apprehensions and become vulnerable and free. Once you do, I promise that you'll have a ton of fun goofing around.

You will probably want to close the curtains before you start. Or not — you do what you feel comfortable doing. Similarly, you can do this while you're home alone, or you can involve your partner or spouse for even more fun! Choose music you enjoy, preferably something upbeat that is easy to dance to. If dancing naked seems too scary, start with your clothes on. Then you can take them off once you have been dancing for a few minutes.

The feeling of being free and releasing all thoughts of who's looking, or what do I look like or what's bouncing or not bouncing, can be eliminated. This is your time to turn the music up loud, sing, and boogie. At first, just do it for a few minutes. If you feel inspired to continue, go for it!

What matters is you enjoy doing it and that you let go of your inhibitions.

You don't have to do this on a regular basis. Personally, I don't, but honestly, I have done it enough to know how incredible the feeling is. I feel so liberated, free, and energetic. There is absolutely no doubt you will feel so much happier not only while you are dancing, but when you are finished. Whenever you need a pick-me-up, dancing naked will do the trick!

Being naked makes the majority of us feel insecure and bashful, but the truth of the matter is that we are all designed the same. We are all beautiful human beings who have our own stories to tell and who all deserve a life of unobstructed happiness. What dancing naked in your living room does is it immediately turns on the happy side of your brain.

We all feel the pressure of such fast-paced lives, which leaves us susceptible to stress, depression and unhealthy choices. Having the ability to strip ourselves down to our core, to become completely vulnerable and to privately dance to some great music not only reduces our stress, but also changes our mood, mindset and increases our self-esteem and positive energy. Dancing naked should be on every doctor's prescription pad!

When your happy brain is turned on you can problem solve better, you can counteract negative emotions, and you can protect your health by lowering your blood pressure and reducing stress. So, the next time you come home from work all fired up, or you have finally got the kids to bed after they have been driving you crazy, close the blinds, turn on your favourite dance song, strip off and get bopping.

Moving and dancing your body can be directly beneficial to your state of mind and happiness. Happiness comes from within you, from realizing that you have control over the way you think about what's going on around you. It is a continual cycle, where your mind drives your body and yet your body drives your mind, so while it is true we change from the inside out, we also change from the outside in.

We become more and more self-conscious and overthink far too much. Keep yourself constantly growing, moving and outside your safe place. The search for happiness is much closer than you know, but for this to happen we must engage our mind, body and spirit. We must be open to having spontaneous, uninhibited fun to truly experience the joy and happiness we all deserve and desire.

 If you are not too sure what to dance to check out this playlist I love on iTunes, just click the link and download straight to your device.

bit.ly/HappinessRescueHAVEFUNPlaylist

AFTERWORD

I sincerely hope this book has provided you with some incredible value; insight, information and motivation that will help you achieve greater happiness in your life. I also hope that this book continues to be a trusted companion on your journey and you will recommend it to any of your friends, family and colleagues who may need support.

You might be feeling a little overwhelmed. If you're wondering where to start, I suggest doing 3 things that will provide you immediate benefits on your Happiness Rescue journey.

1. **Please reflect back to Chapter 17 where we discussed meditation.**
   Meditation is one ritual you can begin to implement into your life immediately and to receive life-altering insight from. To start, please go to: bit.ly/HappinessWithinYou10min and download my personal *Happiness is Within You* guided meditation. It is 10 minutes in length, which is a fantastic starting point for newbies and a simple reminder meditation for those who are more experienced. Reread the

meditation chapter to make sure you are comfortable with how to meditate and proceed with your first meditation practice.

Commit to meditating for sixty days. Continue to use the *Happiness Within You* guided practice until you feel comfortable enough to try a longer guided meditation or a silent meditation session. It takes sixty days to build a ritual into your life, as discussed in chapter 14 about setting goals and establishing rituals.

2. **Sign-up for the Amanda May Stark email list.**
The best lessons we learn in life are the ones we learn over and over again. Your experience with me does not have to end with this book. You can take immediate action by filling in your information so you can receive weekly blog posts to help you live a happy and self-empowered life.

In my emails, you will find a lot of ideas and strategies you can continue to implement into your life on a continual basis. We never stop growing and I do not want to stop helping and inspiring you along your happiness journey. I am constantly exploring exciting ways to live a phenomenal life and I'm excited to always be able to share them with you.

If you want to keep your mind, body, and spirit inspired, and continue taking action toward an inspired, happy life, please sign up at www.amandamaystark.com.

3. **Join the SMILE for Women Facebook Group.**
   This group is for women who are seeking greater success, mindfulness, inspiration, love and empowerment in their lives. It is where you'll find daily inspiration, connect with others and dive deeper into creating the life you envision. It is the perfect place for like-minded people who are striving for a happier, healthier fulfilled life. It is here you may share your stories, struggles, and victories while being supported by others who are all aspiring for the same goal… their personal happiness.

   This is a closed group for my clients and readers. When you submit your request to join, please answer the questions and mention you are a Happiness Rescue reader.

   Find it at: facebook.com/groups/smileforwomen

CONTINUE YOUR HAPPINESS RESCUE WITH ME!

"To be happy is your decision, not anyone else's. The sooner you step up and decide you've had enough of walking in your own shadow is the time to take action. Begin your journey towards your own happiness rescue without delay or second-thoughts, but with conviction, intention and faith."
~ Amanda Stark ~

Happiness Rescue has been a labour of love for me as it has pushed me to open myself up to being vulnerable and exposed. I honestly believe for us to grow and evolve we must lower our defences, listen to our hearts, and share our stories with the world.

We do not live in a pretentious world, but a world where we can help one another when required. We live in a world where we can learn from each other's experiences, embrace each other's difficulties, and celebrate each other's successes.

PERSONAL COACHING

If you desire a personal approach to reaching your goals, finding your passion and living your best-fulfilled life, then I can offer you one-on-one personal coaching. In our sessions we work together over a 3, 6 or 12-month period and make your vision your reality. Planning, breaking your boundaries, eliminating your fears and building the confidence you need in order to SMILE (to be successful, mindful, inspired, loved and empowered)!

Personal coaching is the fastest, most productive way to getting what it is you desire in your life. If this is the approach you prefer be prepared to dive deep into places you may not have explored in years! I will be your coach, mentor, and accountability partner through your happiness journey.

There are only a select number of clients I work with each year, so please reach out to me now to get the process started www.amandamaystark.com.

KEYNOTE & GUEST SPEAKING SERIES

SMILE for Women is a sought-after speaking program and is the perfect opportunity for your next event. I am so excited to personally be able to bring SMILE for Women to women worldwide! It is a passion of mine to share my story with others and to help them achieve personal and professional breakthroughs in their lives. With a focus on personal empowerment, I cover a range of topics related to overcoming personal and professional adversities and I do so through my compassionate coaching style and my own personal life experience. At your next engagement I can provide a customized keynote speech, seminar or workshop to meet the needs of any group — from corporations to professional organizations and associations. Every program is based on the core elements of the SMILE for Women platform, which is a series of programs, books, courses, and membership related to success, mindfulness, inspiration, love and empowerment of women.

SMILE for WOMEN ACADEMY MEMBERSHIP & ONLINE COURSES

Commencing early 2019, and expanding from the SMILE for Women speaking series, I offer online courses and a membership program. The courses vary from self-paced programs through to programs containing group and private coaching. The online initiative is designed for people seeking greater success, mindfulness, inspiration, love and empowerment in their lives.

The SMILE for Women Academy is *the* breakthrough platform for anyone serious about taking action. We do this through a very specific process, which helps you get unstuck, reach your goals, build confidence and create your own happy, healthy, fulfilled life. If you would like to work with me, this is the fastest, most direct and powerful way for you to begin your transformation.

The SMILE for Women Academy is a system that works time and again to break people from their ruts and get them back on track to living a life they are excited about. The platform has proven ways to overcome your self-doubt, conquer your inner bully, skyrocket your goals, foster stronger relationships, and help you let go of painful emotions. The learning modules will inspire you to become your best-empowered self.

When you invest in the SMILE for Women Academy membership, you will receive access to a valuable collection of helpful resources, from inspiring stories to actionable strategies. The SMILE for Women Academy membership offers incredible support from an uplifting community that you can lean on, exchange information with, and grow from.

Learn more about the SMILE for Women Academy at: www.amandamaystark.com

EVERYDAY HAPPINESS - UNLOCK THE HAPPINESS YOU DESERVE

I know how hard it can be to make the decision to change your life, so I have one more special gift for you. In my previously published eBook, I talk about everyday happiness and other areas you can consider when creating your own happiness rescue. Simply go to my website at amandamaystark.com and find the yellow happy face book cover titled "Everyday Happiness - Unlock the Happiness You Deserve." Fill in your information and download it right to your computer.

It will help you define, design and create the life you deserve and desire.

It Starts with a SMILE ☺

Amanda Stark
Mindset & Well-Being Coach

REDISCOVER YOUR PASSION WORKSHEET

Rediscover Your Passion Worksheet

5 Powerful Steps to Rediscovering Your Passion and Living a Purposeful and Happy Life

NAME: _____ DATE: _____

RECOMMENDED Reading:

- "Start with Why" by Simon Sinek
- "The Passion Test" by Janet Bray & Chris Attwood

1. BRAINSTORMING

Start by brainstorming all the passions, hobbies and activities you had as a child/teenager that brought you joy. There are no limits here, nothing silly, just start writing. Try to come up with at least 10. The more the merrier. Some examples to help your process may be: soccer, music, sewing, make-up, fashion, animals, cooking, helping people, painting, pottery, writing, chess, tennis, etc.

1. _____
2. _____
3. _____
4. _____

5. _____

6. _____

7. _____

8. _____

9. _____

10. _____

2. PICK YOUR TOP 3

It is time to narrow it down. Choose your top 3 favourites, which stand out as the most interesting and exciting choices for your life as it is right now. Make sure these are your choices and you haven't been swayed by anyone else. For you to rediscover your true passions, they must be yours and not those of others.

1. _____

2. _____

3. _____

3. WHY ARE THEY SO IMPORTANT TO YOU?

Write 3 ways each passion is most valuable to you. REMEMBER: Be very specific, DIG DEEP into the emotion of what you really feel for each one. Keep what you feel other people will feel about it separate, this is specifically how you feel!

First Passion

1. _____

2. _____

3. _____

Second Passion

1. _____

2. _____

3. _____

Third Passion

1. _____

2. _____

3. _____

4. CHOOSE ONE & COMMIT

Now it is getting more challenging, but don't over think this. **Choose just ONE.** This should be **THE MOST EXCITING ONE**, which stands out to you. Get clear and avoid mixed signals. You cannot choose more than one, as we want to focus and give ourselves the best opportunity to embrace our rediscovered passion back into our life. Make sure you feel it in your gut; "that is called your intuition." It will never fail you.

1. _____

5. PUT YOUR PASSION INTO ACTION

Now that you have decided on the passion you are going to focus on and you know what action steps need to happen, it is time to plan your attack. We want to be proactive in this and not delay any action to implementing your passion into your schedule and your life.

Grab your digital, wall mount or desktop calendar and pen it in. I use a pen, so it is less likely to be deleted from my schedule. Book the class, time-block practice sessions and really commit to the process of learning and implementing your new passion into your routine.

This is also about scheduling time in for yourself. The time you spend concentrating on your passion is your special "me time" and should always be a priority moving forward. Like your family, your job, and all of your other responsibilities, making time for you is as important and worth investing in.

FURTHER COACHING

CONGRATULATIONS for completing the **Rediscover Your Passion Worksheet!**

Now it's time to progress you to the next level in your life!

I invite you to take keep the momentum going as I have limited spots available in my personal coaching program. This is where we expand on what you have accomplished so far and reach into other areas of your life.

Type **"Passion Discovery"** in the email subject line and take action TODAY!

Amanda Stark
Mindset & Well-Being Coach
Amanda@amandamaystark.com
Your SMILE Specialist and Happiness Rescue Expert
Helping you Rediscover, Reclaim, and Recreate Happiness in Your Life.

ACKNOWLEDGEMENTS

"A strong marriage rarely has two strong people at the same time. It is a husband and wife who take turns being strong for each other in the moments when the other feels weak."
~ Ashley Willis ~

This book has come from years of thinking. Years of thinking "I'd like to write a book." And years of listening to my inner bully telling me: "You don't have the skills to write a book."

Leading up to writing this book, I experienced the most numbing, sometimes debilitating sense of loss. While I have always battled my own insecurities, I could usually hide them behind my purpose or my identity, which was always my job and my children.

Within the course of 18 months I suddenly lost my job, our home became an empty nest, and suddenly I had no purpose in my life. Searching under every rock, pebble and grain I tried desperately to discover my next life passion and purpose, but the only thing I ever came up with was spent money and lost hope.

Meanwhile, while I was trying to keep myself afloat I didn't realize it, but I was sinking in quick sand. Every day, I was getting sucked in deeper and deeper until one day I almost stopped breathing. Ironically, this was the day I was rescued and I reached out for help.

I had to get to my lowest to realize I was not super human and I could not do it on my own. Ironically, while I was so caught up in the darkness I didn't realize it, but I had never been alone at all. For while, I was living within the darkness, my adoring husband was right by my side, living each day with me. Throughout all the tears, self-pity, failures, and moderate successes, he was always there.

The message here is just when you think you are alone, you are not. Open your eyes, ask for help, and do not wait until you are so deep you cannot see the sun.

This book was born from one magical moment at my oldest son's wedding, where I saw the sun for the first time in years. I am so grateful for that moment in my life and for all those who were with us that incredible day.

Happiness Rescue is dedicated to all of my beautiful family; my sons, their girls, my sister, my parents, our blended family, and my husband, as without his support I could not have written this book.

Glenn, you have had my back for the past twelve years and I am so grateful we have a lifetime of happiness ahead of us. Throughout this process you have been my rock, my confidant, our domestic engineer, and our errand boy as you have picked up so much slack around our home and made us function, when I was not functioning.

Thank you my love, for always having my best interest, for putting up with the darkest days, and for embracing my ambition to become an author.

James Glenn Stark, this book is for US with love!

Amanda xx

ABOUT THE AUTHOR

Amanda May Stark is a wife, mother, daughter, her own boss, mindset and well-being coach, entrepreneur, author, and an ocean loving girl.

Overcoming MANY life obstacles, she is an EXPERT in overcoming adversity and making lemonade from lemons.

With many pinnacle life experiences and overcoming many difficult life adversities, Amanda brings to the table a very different approach to her coaching and writing. She is honest, genuine, approachable, and vulnerable in her style and communication.

Through her writing, coaching and speaking events, she has spent the past decade embracing life and discovering the SMILE for Women program.

It is through this program, that she can offer you insightful strategies for getting unstuck, reaching your goals, building confidence, and feeling happier.

Amanda will help you define, design and create the life you deserve and desire.

She knows without a strong coach by your side, distraction and focus can be factors that over time if not managed, can lead to failure.

Life does NOT need to be an uphill climb. Amanda is your SMILE Specialist and Happiness Rescue expert... lean on her and together you will have fun and get your happy back!

Amanda lives in Calgary, Canada with her husband Glenn and their fur-companions. As an empty nester, her two sons and daughter-in-law live nearby and can be persuaded to pop over as long as dinner and a hot tub are on the menu.

She enjoys long walks with her dogs, spending time with family, beach vacations, movie nights with Glenn and a good glass of wine.

www.amandamaystark.com

Amanda May Stark Facebook Page: facebook.com/amandamaystark

SMILE for Women Facebook Group: facebook.com/groups/smileforwomen

Made in the USA
Middletown, DE
30 November 2018